National Air Quality

STATUS AND TRENDS THROUGH 2007

U.S. Environmental Protection Agency
Office of Air Quality Planning and Standards
Air Quality Assessment Division
Research Triangle Park, North Carolina

EPA-454/R-08-006
November 2008

Table of Contents

This summary report highlights EPA's most recent evaluation of the status and trends in our nation's air quality.

LEVELS OF SIX COMMON POLLUTANTS CONTINUE TO DECLINE

- Cleaner cars, industries, and consumer products have contributed to cleaner air for much of the U.S.

- Since 1990, nationwide air quality for six air pollutants for which there are national standards has improved significantly. These air pollutants are ground-level ozone (O_3), particle pollution ($PM_{2.5}$ and PM_{10}), lead (Pb), nitrogen dioxide (NO_2), carbon monoxide (CO), and sulfur dioxide (SO_2). Nationally, air pollution was lower in 2007 than 1990 for:
  - 8-hour ozone, by 9 percent
  - annual $PM_{2.5}$ (since 2000), by 11 percent
  - PM_{10}, by 28 percent
  - Lead, by 80 percent
  - NO_2, by 35 percent
  - 8-hour CO, by 67 percent
  - SO_2, by 54 percent

- Despite clean air progress, in 2007, 158.5 million people lived in counties that exceeded any national ambient air quality standard (NAAQS). Ground-level ozone and particle pollution still present challenges in many areas of the country.

- Though $PM_{2.5}$ concentrations were higher in 2007 than in 2006, partly due to weather conditions, annual $PM_{2.5}$ concentrations were nine percent lower in 2007 than in 2001.

- 8-hour ozone concentrations were five percent lower in 2007 than in 2001. Ozone levels did not improve in much of the East until 2002, after which there was a significant decline. This decline is largely due to reductions in oxides of nitrogen (NO_x) emissions required by EPA's rule to reduce ozone in the East, the NO_x SIP Call. EPA tracks progress toward meeting these reductions through its NO_x Budget Trading Program.

LEVELS OF MANY TOXIC AIR POLLUTANTS HAVE DECLINED

- In 2007, 27 National Air Toxics Trends Stations (NATTS) were fully operational, providing a consistent long-term national network operated by state and local agencies with coordination provided by EPA.

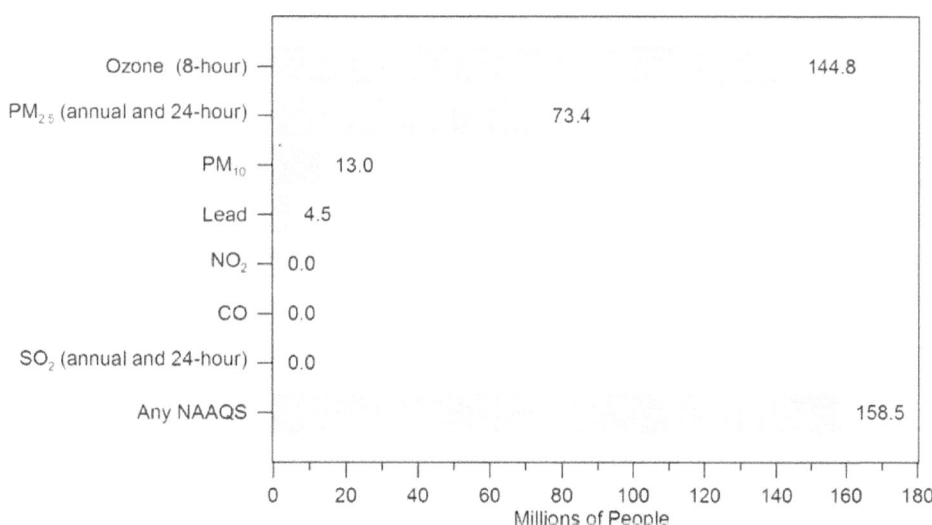

Number of people living in counties with air quality concentrations above the level of the primary (health-based) National Ambient Air Quality Standards (NAAQS) in 2007.

Note: In 2008, EPA strengthened the national standard for 8-hour ozone to 0.075 ppm and the national standard for lead to 0.15 µg/m³. This figure includes people living in counties that monitored ozone and lead concentrations above the new levels. $PM_{2.5}$ are particles less than or equal to 2.5 micrometers (µm) in diameter. PM_{10} are particles less than or equal to 10 µm in diameter.

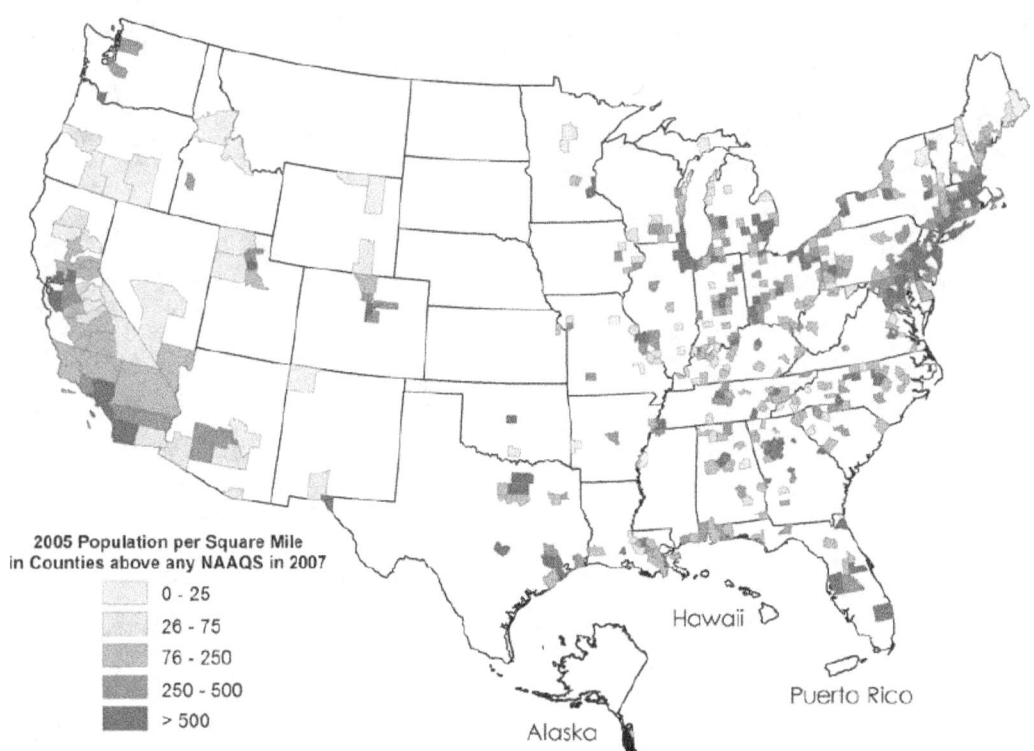

**2005 Population per Square Mile
in Counties above any NAAQS in 2007**

- 0 - 25
- 26 - 75
- 76 - 250
- 250 - 500
- > 500

Hawaii

Puerto Rico

Alaska

Population density (2005 population per square mile) in counties with air quality concentrations above the level of any of the primary NAAQS in 2007.

Note: This figure includes counties that monitored ozone and lead concentrations above the new levels set in 2008.

- Toxic hydrocarbons such as benzene, 1,3-butadiene, styrene, xylenes, and toluene decreased by 5 percent or more per year between 2000 and 2005 at more than half of ambient monitoring sites. Other key contributors to cancer risk, such as carbon tetrachloride, tetrachloroethylene, and 1,4-dichlorobenzene, declined at most sites.

- Control programs for mobile sources and facilities such as chemical plants, dry cleaners, coke ovens, and incinerators are primarily responsible for reductions in toxic air pollutant emissions between 2000 and 2005. These emissions reductions have contributed to reductions in cancer risk as well as reductions in the hydrocarbon contribution to ozone concentrations.

ACID RAIN AND HAZE ARE DECLINING

- EPA's NO_x SIP Call and Acid Rain Program have contributed to significant improvements in air quality and environmental health. The required reductions in sulfur dioxide and oxides of nitrogen have led to significant decreases in atmospheric deposition, contributing to improved water quality in lakes and streams. For example, between the 1989-1991 and 2005-2007 time periods, wet sulfate deposition and wet nitrate deposition decreased more than 30 percent in parts of the East.

- Between 1996 and 2006, visibility in scenic areas has improved throughout the country. Five areas—Mt. Rainier National Park, Wash.; Great Smoky Mountains National Park, Tenn.; Great Gulf Wilderness, N.H.; Canyonlands National Park, Utah; and Snoqualmie Pass, Wash.—show notable improvement on days with the worst visibility.

CLIMATE CHANGE AND INTERNATIONAL TRANSPORT: IMPROVING OUR UNDERSTANDING

- The U.N. Intergovernmental Panel on Climate Change concluded climate change is evident from observations of increases in global average air and ocean temperatures, widespread melting of snow and ice, and rising global average sea level.

- Research is under way to examine and improve our understanding of the links between air quality and climate: how a warming climate could affect air quality and how air quality could affect climate.

- Researchers also are improving our understanding about how pollution moves between countries and continents.

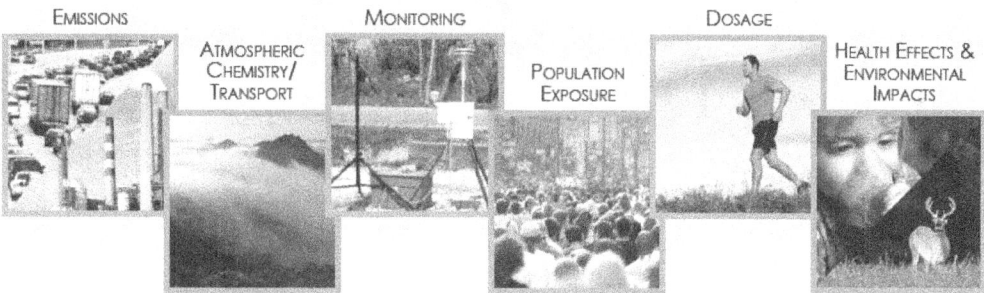

Sources-to-Effects Continuum

EMISSIONS

ATMOSPHERIC CHEMISTRY/ TRANSPORT

MONITORING

POPULATION EXPOSURE

DOSAGE

HEALTH EFFECTS & ENVIRONMENTAL IMPACTS

Because air pollution harms human health and damages the environment, EPA tracks pollutant emissions. Air pollutants are emitted from a variety of sources including stationary fuel combustion, industrial processes, highway vehicles, and non-road sources. These pollutants react in and are transported through the atmosphere. EPA, other federal agencies, and state, local, and tribal agencies monitor air quality at locations throughout the U.S. Data collected through ambient monitoring are used in models to estimate population exposure. Personal health monitoring is conducted via special studies to better understand actual dosage of pollutants. EPA uses monitoring data, population exposure estimates, and personal dosage data to better understand health effects and environmental impacts of air pollutants.

MORE IMPROVEMENTS ANTICIPATED

- EPA expects air quality to continue to improve as recent regulations are fully implemented and states work to meet national standards. Among these regulations are: the Locomotive Engines and Marine Compression - Ignition Engines Rule, the Tier II Vehicle and Gasoline Sulfur Rule, the Heavy-Duty Highway Diesel Rule, the Clean Air Non-road Diesel Rule, and the Mobile Source Air Toxics Rule.

HEALTH AND ENVIRONMENTAL IMPACTS

Air pollution can affect our health in many ways. Numerous scientific studies have linked air pollution to a variety of health problems including (1) aggravation of respiratory and cardiovascular disease (as indicated by increased emergency department visits and hospital admissions); (2) decreased lung function and increased frequency and severity of respiratory symptoms such as difficulty breathing and coughing; (3) increased susceptibility to respiratory infections; (4) effects on the nervous system, including the brain, such as IQ loss and impacts on learning, memory, and behavior; (5) cancer; and (6) premature death. Some sensitive individuals appear to be at greater risk for air pollution-related health effects, for example, those with pre-existing heart and lung diseases (e.g., asthma, emphysema, and chronic bronchitis), diabetics, older adults, and children. In 2007, 158.5 million people lived in counties that exceeded national air quality standards.

Air pollution also damages our environment. Ozone can damage vegetation including adversely impacting the growth of trees and reducing crop yields. Visibility is reduced by particle pollutants that scatter and absorb light. Typical visual range in the eastern U.S. is 15 to 30 miles, approximately one-third of what it would be without man-made air pollution. In the West, the typical visual range is about 60 to 90 miles, or about one-half of the visual range under natural conditions.

Pollution in the form of acids and acid-forming compounds (such as sulfur dioxide [SO_2] and oxides of nitrogen [NO_x]) can deposit from the atmosphere to the Earth's surface. This is called acid deposition and can be either dry or wet. Wet deposition is more commonly known as acid rain. Acid rain can occur anywhere and, in some areas, rain can be 100 times more acidic than natural precipitation. Acid deposition can be a very serious regional problem, particularly in areas downwind from high SO_2 and NO_x emitting sources, e.g., coal burning power plants, smelters, and factories. Acid deposition can have many harmful ecological effects in both land and water systems. While acid deposition can damage tree foliage directly, it more commonly stresses trees by changing the chemical and physical characteristics of the soil. In lakes, acid deposition can kill fish and other aquatic life.

The burning of fossil fuels, such as coal and oil, and deforestation can cause concentrations of heat-trapping "greenhouse gases" to increase significantly in our atmosphere. These gases prevent heat from escaping to space, somewhat like the glass panels of a greenhouse. Greenhouse gases are necessary to life as we know it, because they keep the planet's surface warmer than it would otherwise be. But, as the concentrations of these gases continue to increase in the atmosphere, the Earth's temperature is climbing above past levels. Studies show that growth in greenhouse gases and associated changes in weather conditions may increase current air pollution levels.

Air Pollution and Health/Welfare Effects – Improving Our Knowledge

Air pollution continues to have adverse impacts on the human and environmental health of the United States, despite clear evidence that overall air quality has improved. EPA's research program is evolving with growing emphasis on the development of a multi-pollutant approach for assessing the impacts of air pollution. Critical components of this research will inform our understanding of how pollutants from sources impact ambient air concentrations, how these concentrations relate to exposures, and, in turn, how exposures relate to health and welfare outcomes. Some highlights of current air pollution research activities include:

- EPA-funded **Particulate Matter Research Centers** are conducting cutting-edge research to improve our understanding of how particle pollution affects human health and the sources of particles most responsible for these effects. Research grants focus high-priority issues including human susceptibility, mechanisms of health effects, exposure-response relationships, and the cross-cutting issue of linking health effects with particle pollution sources and components.

- The **Multi-Ethnic Study of Atherosclerosis and Air Pollution (MESA Air)** is investigating the impact of air pollution on the progression of cardiovascular disease among more than 7,000 participants with diverse backgrounds from nine locations. The study will help evaluate if cardiac disease is accelerated by exposure to particle pollution in combination with gaseous pollutants and if some ethnic populations are more susceptible to effects associated with these exposures.

- The **Health Effects Institute's National Particle Components Toxicity (NPACT) Initiative** will build upon the existing scientific foundation for particles to improve our understanding of the toxicity of specific components and characteristics of particle pollution (and ultimately sources of these components).

Air Pollution Sources, Health Effects, and Environmental Effects

Pollutant	Sources	Health Effects	Environmental Effects
Ozone (O_3)	Secondary pollutant formed by chemical reaction of VOCs and NO_x in the presence of sunlight.	Aggravation of respiratory and cardiovascular disease, decreased lung function and increased respiratory symptoms, increased susceptibility to respiratory infection, and premature death.	Damage to vegetation such as impacts on tree growth and reduced crop yields.
Particles	Emitted or formed through chemical reactions (e.g., NO_x, SO_2, NH_3); fuel combustion (e.g., burning coal, wood, diesel); industrial processes; agriculture (plowing, field burning); and unpaved roads.	Aggravation of respiratory and cardiovascular disease, reduced lung function, increased respiratory symptoms, and premature death.	Impairment of visibility, effects on climate, and damage and/or discoloration of structures and property.
Lead	Smelters (metal refineries) and other metal industries; combustion of leaded gasoline in piston engine aircraft; waste incinerators; and battery manufacturing.	Damage to developing nervous system, resulting in IQ loss and impacts on learning, memory, and behavior in children. Cardiovascular and kidney effects in adults and early effects related to anemia.	Harm to environment and wildlife.
Sulfur Dioxide (SO_2)	Fuel combustion (especially high-sulfur coal); electric utilities and industrial processes; and natural sources such as volcanoes.	Aggravation of asthma and increased respiratory symptoms. Contributes to particle formation with associated health effects.	Contributes to the acidification of soil and surface water and mercury methylation in wetland areas. Contributes to particle formation with associated environmental effects.
Oxides of Nitrogen (NO_x)	Fuel combustion (e.g., electric utilities, industrial boilers, and vehicles) and wood burning.	Aggravation of respiratory disease and increased susceptibility to respiratory infections. Contributes to ozone and particle formation with associated health effects.	Contributes to the acidification and nutrient enrichment (eutrophication, nitrogen saturation) of soil and surface water. Contributes to ozone and particle formation with associated environmental effects.
Carbon Monoxide (CO)	Fuel combustion (especially vehicles).	Reduces the ability of blood to carry oxygen to body tissues including vital organs. Aggravation of cardiovascular disease.	None known.
Ammonia (NH_3)	Livestock agriculture (i.e., raising/maintaining livestock for milk, meat, and egg production); fertilizer application.	Contributes to particle formation with associated health effects.	Contributes to eutrophication of surface water and nitrate contamination of ground water. Contributes to particle formation with associated environmental effects.
Volatile Organic Compounds (VOCs)	Fuel combustion and evaporation (especially vehicles); solvents; paint; and natural sources such as trees and vegetation.	Cancer (from some toxic air pollutants) and other serious health problems. Contributes to ozone formation with associated health effects.	Contributes to ozone formation with associated environmental effects.
Mercury	Fuel combustion (especially coal-fired power plants); waste disposal; industrial processes; mining; and natural sources (volcanoes and evaporation from enriched soil, wetlands, and oceans).	Liver, kidney, and brain damage; and neurological and developmental damage.	Deposition into rivers, lakes, and oceans accumulates in fish resulting in exposure to humans and wildlife.
Other Toxic Air Pollutants	Fuel combustion (including particle and gaseous emissions); vehicles; industrial processes; building materials; and solvents.	Cancer, immune system damage, neurological, reproductive, developmental, respiratory, and other health problems. Some toxic air pollutants contribute to ozone and particle pollution with associated health effects.	Harmful to wildlife and livestock. Some toxic air pollutants accumulate in the food chain. Some toxic air pollutants contribute to ozone and particle pollution with associated environmental effects.

SOURCES OF AIR POLLUTION

Air pollution consists of gas and particle contaminants ($PM_{2.5}$ and PM_{10}) that are present in the atmosphere. Gaseous pollutants include SO_2, NO_x, ozone (O_3), carbon monoxide (CO), volatile organic compounds (VOCs), certain toxic air pollutants, and some gaseous forms of metals. Particle pollution includes a mixture of compounds. The majority of these compounds can be grouped into four categories: sulfates, nitrates, elemental carbon, organic carbon, and "crustal" material.

Some pollutants are compounds that are released directly into the atmosphere. These include gases such as SO_2 and some particles, such as soil and soot. Other pollutants are formed in the air. Ground-level ozone forms when emissions of NO_x and VOCs react in the presence of sunlight. Similarly, some particles are formed. For example, particle sulfates are the product of SO_2 and ammonia (NH_3) gases reacting in the atmosphere. Weather plays an important role in the formation of air pollutants, as discussed later in the ozone and particle pollution sections.

EPA tracks direct emissions of air pollutants and emissions that contribute to air pollution formation, also known as precursor emissions. Emissions data are compiled from many different organizations, including industry and state, tribal, and local agencies. Some emissions data are based on actual measurements while others are estimates.

Emissions, in general, are emitted from large stationary fuel combustion sources (such as electric utilities and industrial boilers), industrial and other processes (such as metal smelters, petroleum refineries, manufacturing facilities, and solvent utilization), and mobile sources including highway vehicles and non-road sources (such as mobile equipment, marine vessels, aircraft, and locomotives). Sources emit different combinations of pollutants. For example, electric utilities release SO_2, NO_x, and particles. Figure 1 shows the distribution of national total emissions estimates by source category for specific pollutants for 2007. Highway vehicles and non-road mobile sources together contribute approximately three-fourths of national CO emissions. Electric utilities contribute about 70 percent of national SO_2 emissions. Agricultural operations (other processes) contribute nearly 80 percent of national NH_3 emissions. Almost 50 percent of the national VOC emissions are coming from highway vehicles and solvent use (other processes). Pollutant levels differ across regions of the country and within local areas, both urban and rural, depending on the size and type of sources present.

The Clean Air Act and EPA have established a list of 187 air toxics (also known as hazardous air pollutants—HAPs). These pollutants are known or are suspected of causing serious health effects, such as cancer, birth defects, or reproductive effects. Many of the VOCs (e.g., benzene, 1,3-butadiene, and chloroform) and particles (e.g., arsenic, lead, and manganese) are toxic air pollutants, as shown in Figure 2.

A number of sources (e.g., stationary fuel combustion, industrial processes, mobile sources) emit both particle and gaseous toxic air pollutants that contribute to both ozone and particle formation. For example, diesel exhaust contains particles as well as VOCs, some of which are toxic.

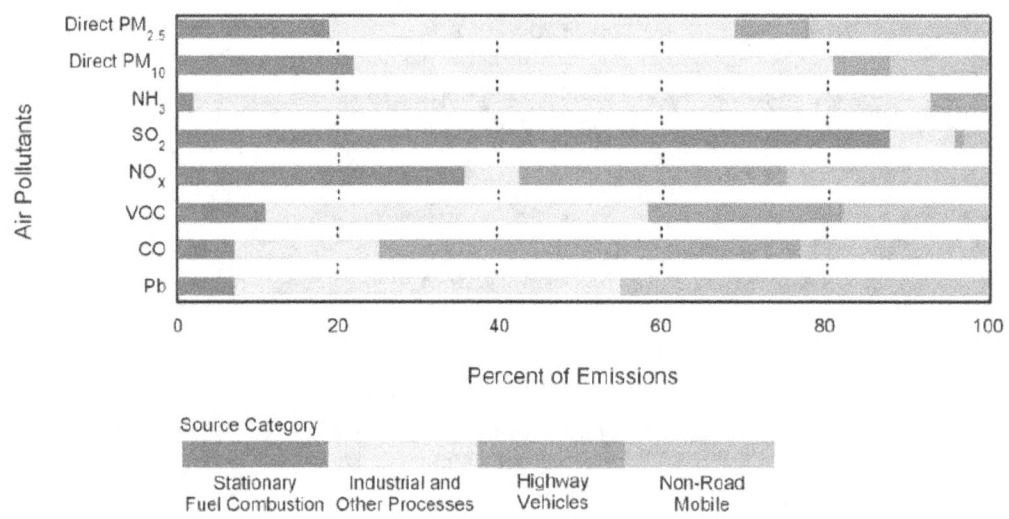

Figure 1. Distribution of national total emissions by source category for specific pollutants, 2007.

Most toxic air pollutants come from a variety of source types. For example, though most benzene emissions are from highway vehicles, benzene is also emitted by some stationary fuel combustion, industrial, and non-road mobile sources.

Control programs that target specific source types can provide multiple benefits. For example, lowering VOC emissions from vehicle sources reduces toxic air pollutant levels and also reduces VOCs that contribute to ozone formation. Lowering NO_x emissions from electric utilities and industrial boilers reduces the NO_x contribution to both ozone and nitrate particle formation, both of which contribute to smog and reduced visibility.

Energy production and transportation sources contribute to CO_2, VOC, SO_2, and NO_x emissions which affect greenhouse gases and the formation of ozone and particle pollution. Reducing energy consumption and vehicle use, or converting to alternative or more efficient energy sources will improve health protection and reduce environmental effects.

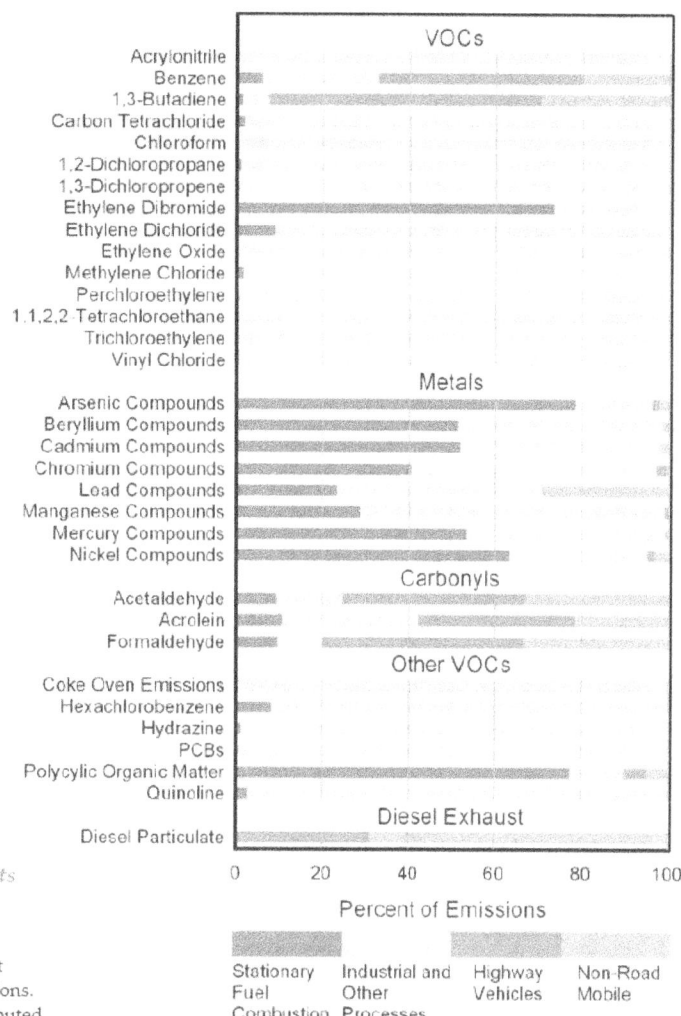

Figure 2. Distribution of national total emissions by source category for individual urban toxic air pollutants and diesel particle pollution, 2005.

Note: Contributions of aldehyde emissions (formaldehyde and acetaldehyde) are for primary direct emissions and do not include secondary aldehydes formed via photochemical reactions. Contributions from fires are not included. In 2005, fires contributed roughly 35 percent of the polycyclic organic matter, 15 percent of the benzene, 37 percent of the 1,3-butadiene, 50 percent of the formaldehyde, 67 percent of the acrolein, and 24 percent of the acetaldehyde.

Emissions Included in this Report

- PM emissions are directly emitted particles only. They do not include gaseous emissions that condense in cooler air (i.e., condensibles) or emissions from fires and resuspended dust.

- SO_2, NO_x, VOC, CO, and lead emissions are from human activity sources only.

- NH_3 emissions are primarily from animal livestock operations and are estimated using population data (e.g., cattle, cows, pigs, poultry) and management practices.

- 2007 emissions were derived from the 2005 emissions inventory, except for SO_2 and NO_x emissions, which were derived from measured data from electric utilities.

- Highway vehicle emissions were based on emission measurements from vehicle testing programs.

- Emissions data were compiled using the best methods and measurements available at the time.

TRACKING POLLUTANT EMISSIONS

Since 1990, air pollutant emissions have declined, with the greatest percentage drop in lead emissions. The removal of lead from gasoline used in highway vehicles is primarily responsible for the 72 percent decrease in lead emissions. NH_3 shows the least percentage drop, four percent. While $PM_{2.5}$ emissions have declined by over one half, PM_{10}, NO_x, and VOC emissions have declined by around one third, and SO_2 and CO emissions have declined by more than one-third, as shown in Table 1.

Table 1. Change in annual national emissions per source category (1990 vs. 2007) (thousand tons).

Source Category	$PM_{2.5}$	PM_{10}	NH_3	SO_2	NO_x	VOC	CO	Pb
Stationary Fuel Combustion	-693	-722	+40	-9036	-4894	+621	-207	-0.410
Industrial and Other Processes	-224	-43	-353	-844	+229	-2809	+8442	-2.621
Highway Vehicles	-223	-235	+152	-412	-4029	-5786	-68645	-0.421
Non-road Mobile	-49	-62	-28	-25	+383	-12	-2685	-0.153
Total Change (thousand tons)	-1189	-1062	-189	-10267	-8311	-7986	-63095	-3.604
Percent Change (1990 vs. 2007)	-51%	-33%	-4%	-45%	-33%	-35%	-44%	-72%

Note: Lead (Pb) emission changes are from 1990 to 2002.

The combined emissions of the six common pollutants ($PM_{2.5}$, SO_2, NO_x, VOCs, CO, and lead) dropped 41 percent since 1990, as shown in Figure 3. This progress has occurred while the U.S. economy continued to grow, Americans drove more miles, and population and energy use increased. These emissions reductions resulted from a variety of control programs through regulations and through voluntary partnerships between federal, state, local, and tribal governments; academia; industrial groups; and environmental organizations.

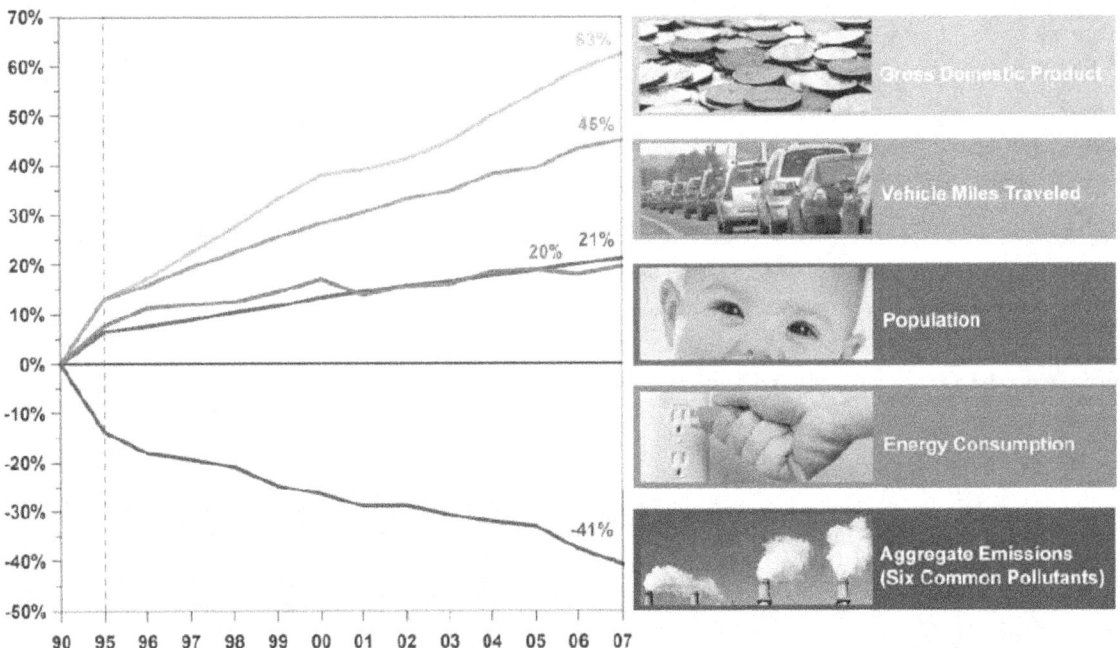

Figure 3. Comparison of growth measures and emissions, 1990-2007.

Note: The U.S. Department of Transportation's Federal Highway Administration reports that cumulative travel for January-April 2008 is down by 2.1 percent compared to the same period in 2007.

Emissions Where You Live

To get emissions information at a state or local level, visit http://www.epa.gov/air/emissions/where.htm. Here you can find emissions totals for a state or county grouped by major source types, or select Google Earth to see nearby sources of emissions. Zoom to the area of interest, tilt the map to see emissions levels, select a site for facility information, or zoom closer for an aerial photo.

Zoom to Atlanta   **Tilt to see emissions levels**   **Select a site**

Aerial photo

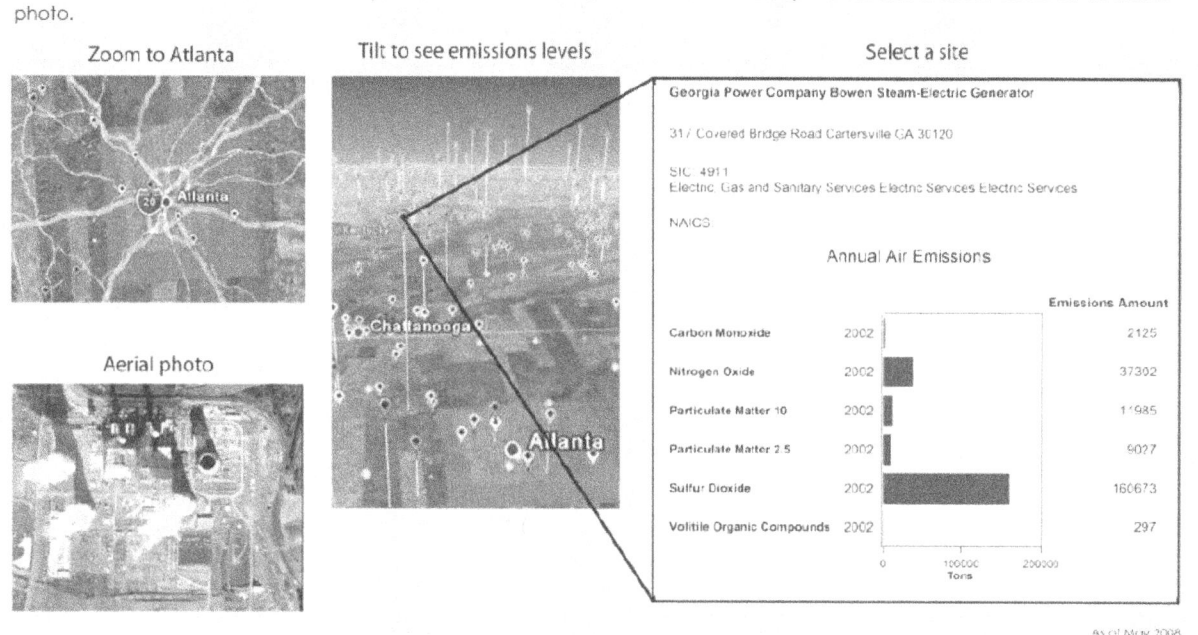

Georgia Power Company Bowen Steam-Electric Generator

317 Covered Bridge Road Cartersville GA 30120

SIC 4911
Electric Gas and Sanitary Services Electric Services Electric Services

NAICS

Annual Air Emissions

		Emissions Amount
Carbon Monoxide	2002	2125
Nitrogen Oxide	2002	37302
Particulate Matter 10	2002	11985
Particulate Matter 2.5	2002	9027
Sulfur Dioxide	2002	160673
Volitile Organic Compounds	2002	297

As of May 2008

SIX COMMON POLLUTANTS

To protect public health and the environment, EPA has established, and regularly reviews, national air quality standards for six common air pollutants also known as "criteria" pollutants: ground-level ozone, particle pollution ($PM_{2.5}$ and PM_{10}), lead, nitrogen dioxide (NO_2), carbon monoxide (CO), and sulfur dioxide (SO_2).

TRENDS IN NATIONAL AIR QUALITY CONCENTRATIONS

Air quality is measured by monitors located across the country. Monitored levels of the six common pollutants show improvement since the Clean Air Act was amended in 1990. Figure 4 shows national trends between 1990 and 2007 in the common pollutants relative to their air quality standards. Most pollutants show a steady decline throughout the time period. Lead declined in the 1990s as control programs were implemented to lower concentrations in areas above

the national standard. In general, lead concentrations have remained low since 2002. Large year-to-year changes shown in lead concentrations reflect the influence of emissions changes due to operating schedules or other facility activities, such as plant closings, on measurements at nearby monitors. Ozone and $PM_{2.5}$ trends are not smooth and show year-to-year influences of weather conditions which contribute to their formation, dispersion, and removal from the air. Ozone was generally level in the 1990s, and showed a notable decline after 2002 mostly due to oxides of nitrogen (NO_x) emission reductions in the East.

Many areas still have air quality problems caused by one or more pollutant. Ozone and particle pollution continue to present air quality challenges throughout much of the U.S., with many monitors measuring concentrations above, or close to, national air quality standards.

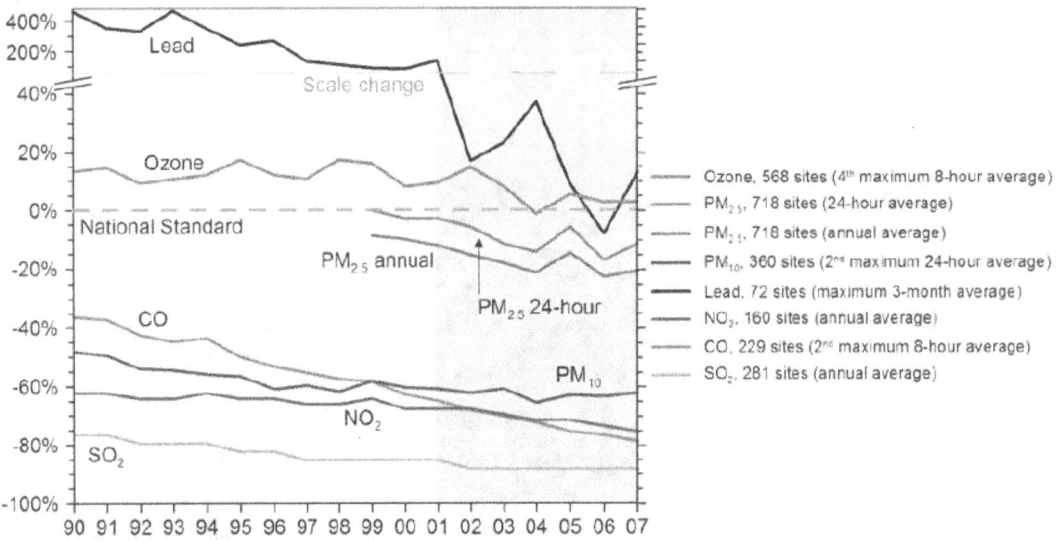

Figure 4. Comparison of national levels of the six common pollutants to national ambient air quality standards, 1990-2007. National levels are averages across all sites with complete data for the time period.

Note: Air quality data for $PM_{2.5}$ start in 1999. Trends from 2001 though 2007 (using the larger number of monitors operating since 2001) are the focus of graphics in the following sections.

Environmental Justice

Environmental justice is the fair treatment and meaningful involvement of all people regardless of race, color, national origin, or income with respect to the development, implementation, and enforcement of environmental laws. EPA's Office of Air and Radiation (OAR) is committed to promoting and supporting environmental justice. For more information about EPA OAR's environmental justice program and air issues, visit http://www.epa.gov/air/ej/.

TRENDS IN "UNHEALTHY" AIR QUALITY DAYS

The Air Quality Index (AQI) relates daily air pollution concentrations for ozone, particles, NO_2, CO, and SO_2 to health concerns for the general public. A value of 100 generally corresponds to the national air quality standard for each pollutant. Values below 100 are generally thought of as satisfactory. Values above 100 are considered to be unhealthy — at first for certain sensitive groups of people, then for everyone as the AQI values increase.

Figure 5 shows the number of unhealthy days that selected metropolitan areas experienced in 2001-2007. Most areas had fewer unhealthy days in 2007 compared to 2001 or 2002. However, Los Angeles, Salt Lake City, and many cities in the east had more unhealthy days in 2007 than in 2006. Nearly all of the increases in unhealthy days in the east are due to ozone and/or particle pollution. Weather conditions, as well as emissions, contribute to ozone and particle pollution formation.

EPA's Air Quality Index (AQI)

Air Quality Index (AQI) Values	Levels of Health Concern
0 to 50	Good
51-100	Moderate
101-150	Unhealthy for Sensitive Groups
151-200	Unhealthy
201-300	Very Unhealthy
301 to 500	Hazardous

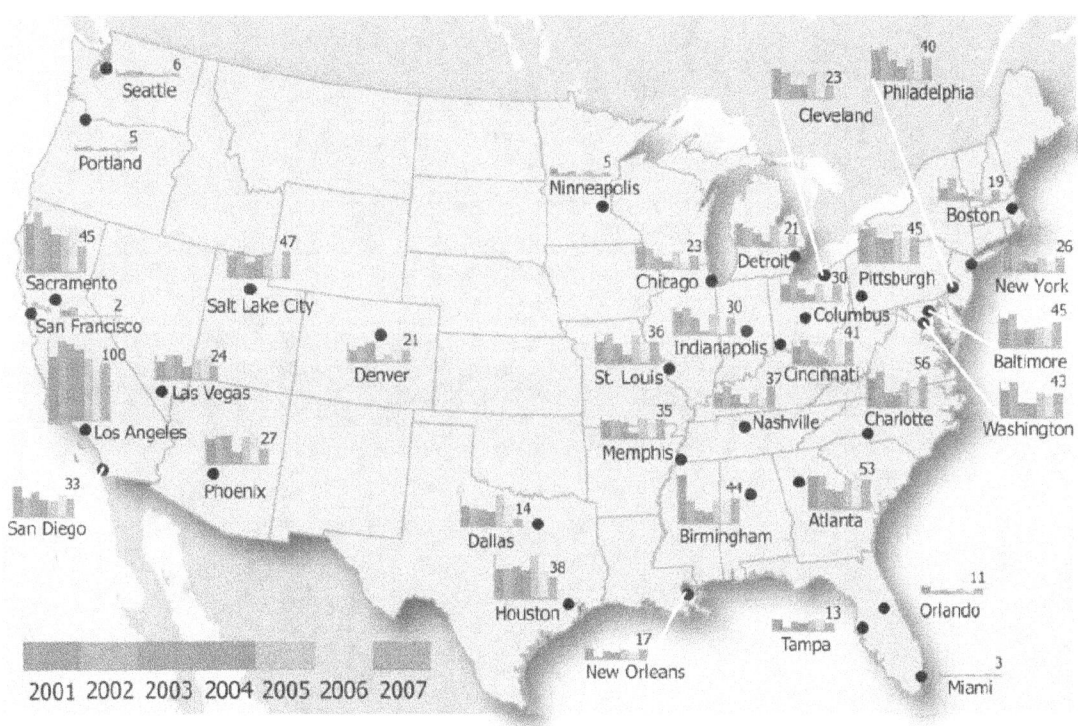

Figure 5. Number of days reaching Unhealthy for Sensitive Groups on the Air Quality Index for 2001-2007 at selected cities.

Note: The AQI breakpoints reflect the new primary standard for 8-hour ozone set in 2008.

Review of the National Ambient Air Quality Standards (NAAQS)

The Clean Air Act requires EPA to set two types of NAAQS for the common air pollutants:

- primary standards to protect public health with an adequate margin of safety, including the health of sensitive populations such as asthmatics, children, and the elderly; and

- secondary standards to protect public welfare from adverse effects, including visibility impairment and effects on the environment (e.g., vegetation, soils, water, and wildlife).

The Clean Air Act requires periodic review of the "standards" and the science upon which they are based. The current standards and the status of each review are shown below.

Pollutant	Primary Standard(s)	Secondary Standard(s)	Status of Review
Ozone	0.075 ppm (8-hour)	Same as Primary	Review completed 2008; the previous 0.08 ppm standard remains in effect
Lead	0.15 µg/m³ (3-month)	Same as Primary	Review completed 2008; the previous 1.5 µg/m³ standard remains in effect
NO_2	0.053 ppm (annual)	Same as Primary	Primary standard review to be completed 2009; secondary standard review of SO_2 and NO_2 to be completed 2010
SO_2	0.03 ppm (annual) 0.14 ppm (24-hour)	0.5 ppm (3-hour)	Primary standard review to be completed 2010; secondary standard review of SO_2 and NO_2 to be completed 2010
$PM_{2.5}$	15 µg/m³ (annual) 35 µg/m³ (24-hour)	Same as Primary	To be completed 2011
PM_{10}	150 µg/m³ (24-hour)	Same as Primary	
CO	9 ppm (8-hour) 35 ppm (1-hour)	None; no evidence of adverse welfare effects at current ambient levels	To be completed 2011

Units of measure are parts per million (ppm) or micrograms per cubic meter of air (µg/m³). For more information about the standards, visit http://www.epa.gov/air/criteria.html.

The Air Quality Management Process

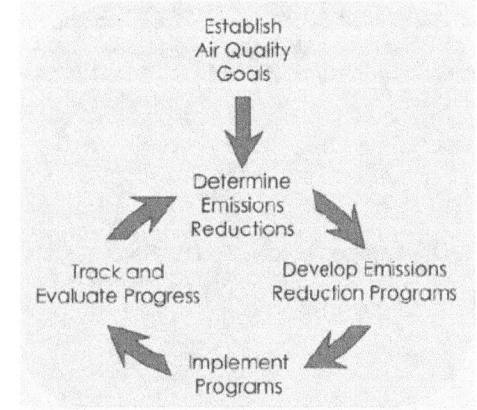

Each time EPA establishes air quality goals necessary to protect public health and the environment, it sets in motion a chain of events. States and local agencies work with EPA to:

- identify emissions reductions needed to achieve air quality goals

- develop emissions reduction programs

- implement emissions reduction strategies and enforcement activities

- track and evaluate progress

AIR QUALITY IN NONATTAINMENT AREAS

Many areas of the country where air pollution levels have exceeded the NAAQS have been designated "nonattainment." Under the Clean Air Act, EPA and state, tribal, and local air quality planning agencies work together to develop plans to address air pollution in these areas. Each year, EPA tracks air quality progress in areas identified as nonattainment by reviewing changes in measured concentrations with respect to the standards. Figure 6 shows which of these areas are above or below one or more of the standards as of 2007.

Air quality has improved in the areas that were designated nonattainment across all six common pollutants. All of the areas designated as nonattainment for CO, SO_2, and NO_2 had air quality levels below their respective standards as of December 2007. Only one of the nonattainment areas was above the standard for lead (1.5 $\mu g/m^3$)—Herculaneum, Mo. For ozone, annual $PM_{2.5}$, and PM_{10}, a number of areas were above the standards: 51, 32, and 17 areas, respectively. Even though many areas were still above the standard in 2007, there have been improvements in the concentration levels in the nonattainment areas. For example, the ozone areas showed a 9 percent improvement, and the annual $PM_{2.5}$ areas showed a 6 percent improvement between the time of designation and 2007.

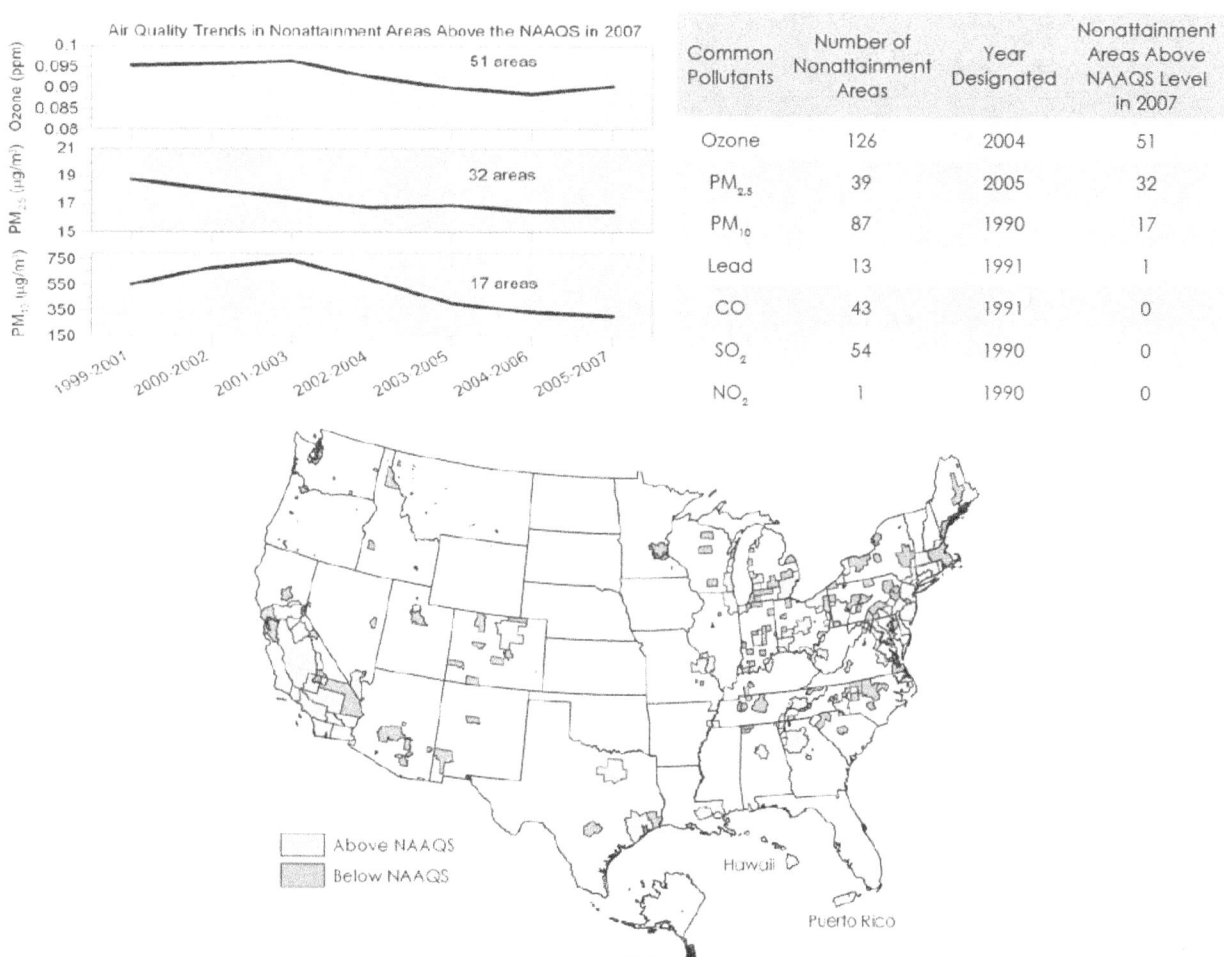

Common Pollutants	Number of Nonattainment Areas	Year Designated	Nonattainment Areas Above NAAQS Level in 2007
Ozone	126	2004	51
$PM_{2.5}$	39	2005	32
PM_{10}	87	1990	17
Lead	13	1991	1
CO	43	1991	0
SO_2	54	1990	0
NO_2	1	1990	0

Figure 6. Status of original nonattainment areas for one or more standards (i.e., 8-hour ozone, maximum quarterly lead, annual $PM_{2.5}$, 24-hour PM_{10}, annual NO_2, 8-hour CO, and annual SO_2) as of 2007.

Notes: Designations for the recently revised standards for ozone (2008), lead (2008), and 24-hour $PM_{2.5}$ (2006) are to be determined. Depending on the form of the standard, a single year or an average of multiple years of data is compared with the level of the standard. For information about air quality standards, visit http://www.epa.gov/air criteria.html. For information about air trends design values, visit http://www.epa.gov/air/airtrends/values.html.

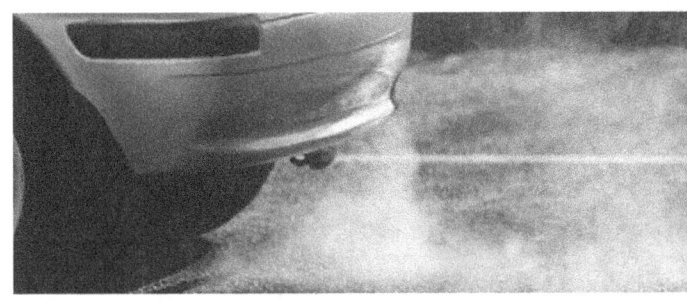

GROUND-LEVEL OZONE

TRENDS IN OZONE CONCENTRATIONS

Nationally, ozone concentrations were 5 percent lower in 2007 than in 2001, as shown in Figure 7. The trend showed a notable decline after 2002. Though concentrations in 2007 were among the lowest since 2002, many areas measured concentrations above the 2008 national

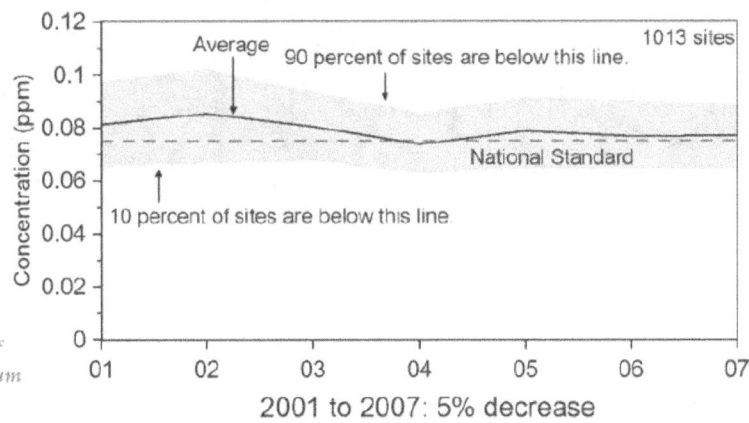

Figure 7. National 8-hour ozone air quality trend, 2001-2007 (average of annual fourth highest daily maximum 8-hour concentrations).

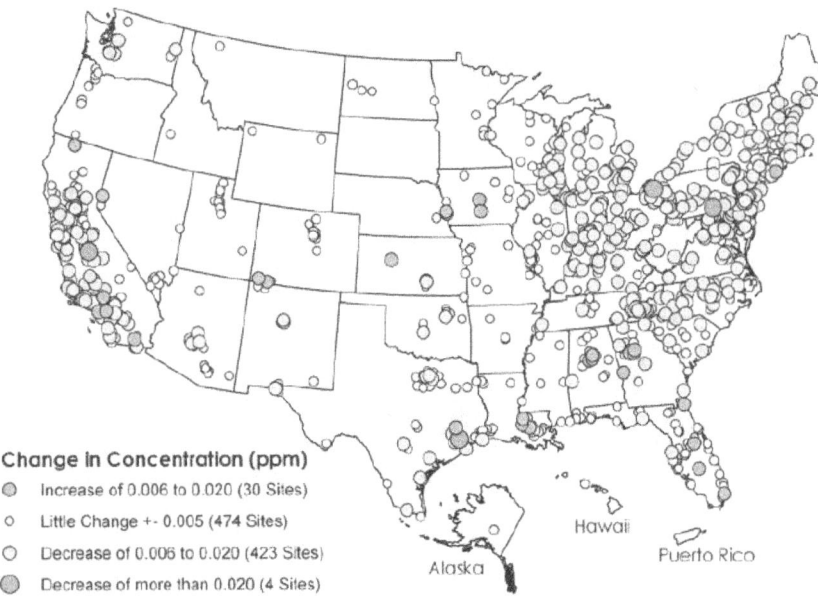

Change in Concentration (ppm)
- Increase of 0.006 to 0.020 (30 Sites)
- Little Change +- 0.005 (474 Sites)
- Decrease of 0.006 to 0.020 (423 Sites)
- Decrease of more than 0.020 (4 Sites)

Figure 8. Change in ozone concentrations in ppm, 2001-2003 vs. 2005-2007 (3-year average of annual fourth highest daily maximum 8-hour concentrations).

air quality standard for ozone (0.075 ppm). When comparing two 3-year periods, 2001-2003 and 2005-2007, 97 percent of the sites show a decline or little change in ozone concentrations as shown in Figure 8. The sites that showed the greatest improvement were in or near the following metropolitan areas: Cleveland, Ohio; parts of Houston, Texas; Fresno, Calif.; and Chambersburg, Pa. However, other parts of Houston also showed a notable increase.

Thirty sites showed an increase of greater than 0.005 ppm. Of the 30 sites that showed an increase, 12 had air quality concentrations below the level of the 2008 ozone standard for the most recent year of data, 2007. The remaining 18 sites with concentrations

EPA Strengthens Ground-level Ozone Standards

On March 12, 2008, EPA strengthened the primary and secondary National Ambient Air Quality Standards for 8-hour ozone to 0.075 ppm. The new standards are tighter than the previous level of 0.08 ppm (effectively 0.084 ppm). The new standards will improve both public health protection and the protection of sensitive trees and plants. Improved health protection includes preventing cases of reduced lung function and respiratory symptoms, acute bronchitis, aggravated asthma, doctor visits, emergency department visits and hospital admissions for individuals with respiratory disease, and premature death in people with heart and lung disease. The Air Quality Index (AQI) breakpoints were changed to reflect the new primary standard. The new 100 AQI level for 8-hour ozone is 0.075 ppm. Information on the AQI can be found at http://www.airnow.gov.

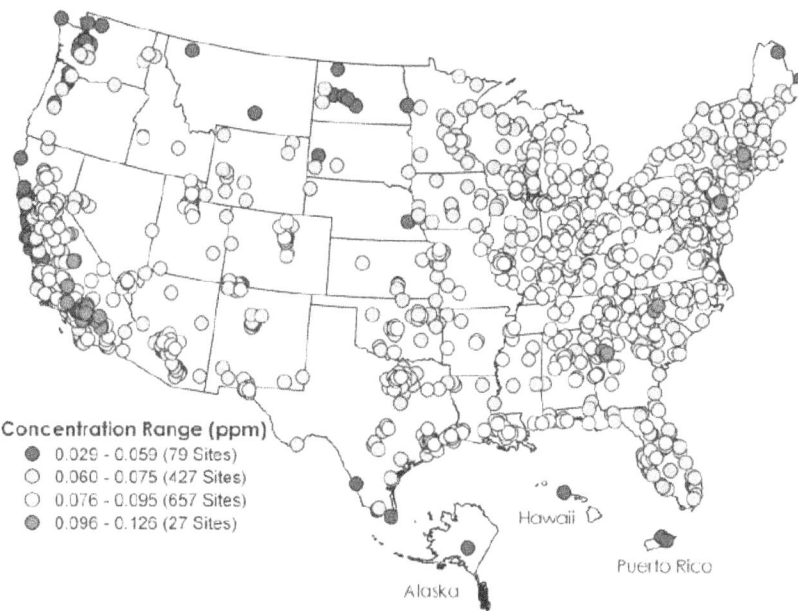

Concentration Range (ppm)
- 0.029 - 0.059 (79 Sites)
- 0.060 - 0.075 (427 Sites)
- 0.076 - 0.095 (657 Sites)
- 0.096 - 0.126 (27 Sites)

Figure 9. Ozone concentrations in ppm, 2007 (fourth highest daily maximum 8-hour concentration).

above the new ozone standard in 2007 were located in or near the following metropolitan areas: Birmingham, Ala.; El Centro, Calif.; Los Angeles, Calif.; Jacksonville, Fla.; Orlando, Fla.; Columbus, Ga.; Atlanta, Ga.; Baton Rouge, La.; New York, N.Y.; and Houston, Texas. Ozone trends can vary locally, as shown by the presence of increases and decreases at nearby sites.

Figure 9 shows a snapshot of ozone concentrations in 2007. The highest ozone concentrations were located in California, Connecticut, Georgia, Massachusetts, North Carolina, and Pennsylvania. Fifty-seven percent of the sites were above 0.075 ppm, the level of the 2008 standard.

EPA Reviews Ozone Monitoring Requirements

EPA is currently reviewing the requirements for ozone monitoring by state and local air agencies. At present, there are about 1200 ozone monitors in operation, mostly in cities with population over 350,000. EPA is reviewing the following aspects of the ozone monitoring program:

- The number of monitors required in smaller cities.
- The number and location of monitors required in rural areas, especially near parks and protected areas.
- The number of months of the year when ozone data must be collected and recorded.

High concentrations of ozone typically occur during months with warm temperatures and strong sunlight. Therefore, year-round monitoring has not been required except in certain areas (see map). Some states monitor in additional months on a voluntary basis. EPA is considering extending the currently required monitoring seasons in light of the new ozone standard level of 0.075 ppm. Data collected during additional months may be necessary to alert the public of all unhealthy days and correctly identify nonattainment areas. For example, 26 of 35 states that are not required to monitor ozone in March do so voluntarily, and in recent years they have measured ozone at unhealthy levels. Similar unhealthy levels may be happening in states not monitoring ozone in March.

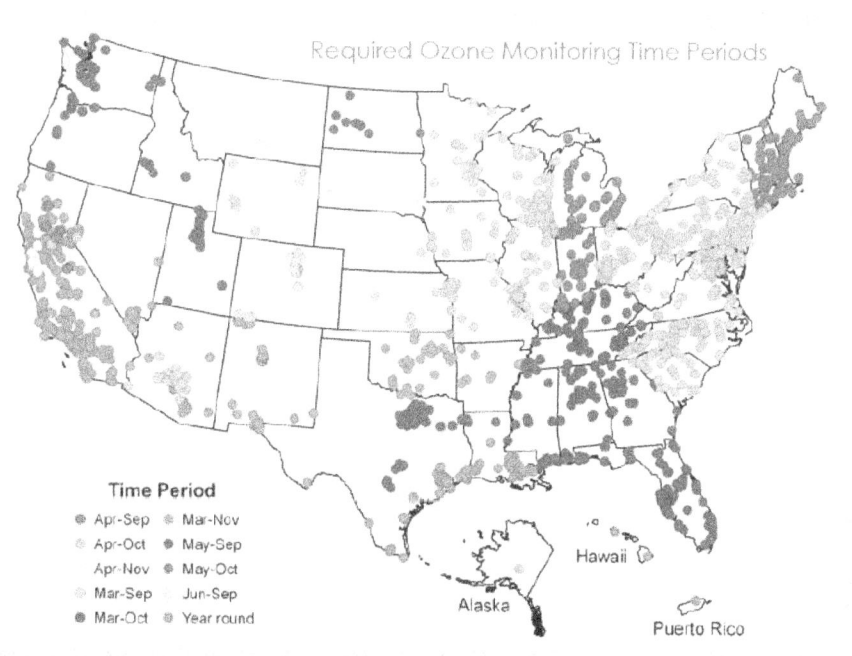

Time Period
- Apr-Sep
- Apr-Oct
- Apr-Nov
- Mar-Sep
- Mar-Oct
- Mar-Nov
- May-Sep
- May-Oct
- Jun-Sep
- Year round

WEATHER CONDITIONS INFLUENCE OZONE

In addition to emissions, weather also plays an important role in the formation of ozone. A large number of hot, dry days can lead to higher ozone levels in any given year, even if ozone-forming emissions do not increase. To better understand how ozone is changing, EPA assesses both the changes in emissions as well as weather conditions. EPA uses a statistical model to calculate a weather adjustment factor that estimates the influence of atypical weather on ozone formation. The adjustment factor is derived from using weather variables such as temperature and humidity. This provides a clearer picture of the underlying pollutant trend from year to year, making it easier to see the effect of changes in emissions on air quality. Geographic differences in the weather adjustment factor for 2007 are shown in Figure 10. In 2007, weather contributed to higher than expected ozone formation in the East, as indicated by values greater than 0.005 ppm.

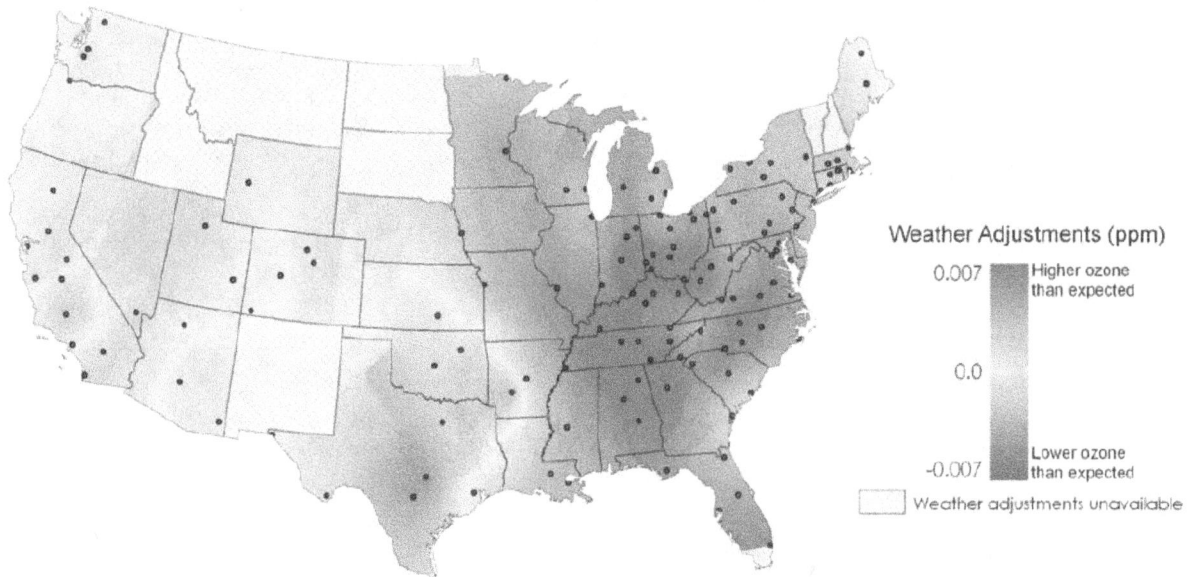

Figure 10. *Difference between 2007 observed and adjusted ozone concentrations (average daily maximum 8-hour ozone for May-September). The map shows areas where weather contributed to higher or lower ozone concentrations than expected. Estimated changes for locations farther from monitoring sites (dots on map) have the largest uncertainty.*

Note: For information on the statistical model, read "The effects of meteorology on ozone in urban areas and their use in assessing ozone trends," by Louise Camalier, William Cox, and Pat Dolwick of the U.S. EPA. *Atmospheric Environment* 41, Pages 7127-7137, 2007.

Figure 11 shows ozone trends for 2001 through 2007, averaged across selected sites before and after adjusting for weather. At the national level, observed ozone levels show a very small decrease of one percent between 2001 and 2007 compared with a larger decrease of eight percent after removing the influence of weather. By examining the data separately for California vs. eastern U.S., it is clear that the majority of the ozone improvement, after adjusting for weather, occurs in the East (on the order of 10 percent).

The largest change in observed and weather adjusted ozone in the East occurred during the period from 2002 through 2004, and was especially noticeable between 2003 and 2004. This relatively abrupt change in ozone levels coincides with the large oxides of nitrogen (NO_x) emissions reductions brought about from implementation of the NO_x SIP Call rule, which began in 2003 and 2004. This significant improvement in ozone continues into 2007, i.e., weather-adjusted levels in 2007 are the lowest over the 7-year period.

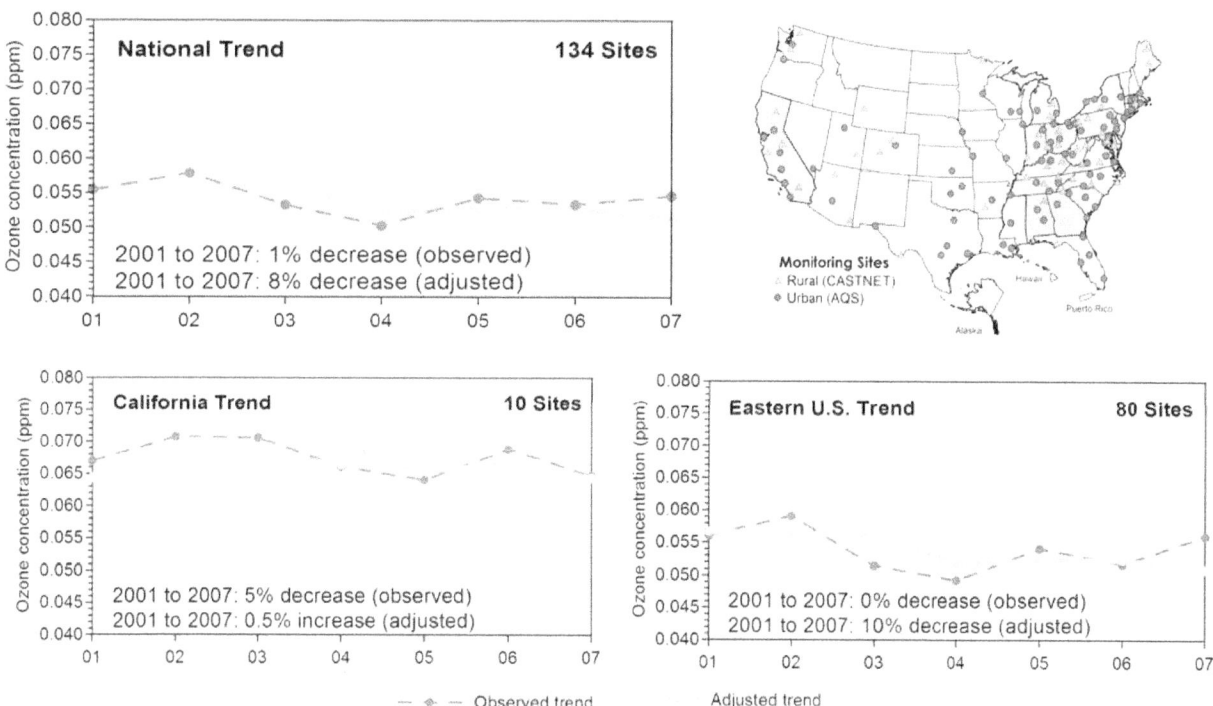

Figure 11. Trends in average summertime daily maximum 8-hour ozone concentrations (May–September), before and after adjusting for weather nationally, in California and in eastern states; and the location of urban and rural monitoring sites used in the averages.

Notes: Urban areas are represented by multiple monitoring sites. Rural areas are represented by a single monitoring site. For more information about the Air Quality System (AQS), visit http://www.epa.gov/ttn/airs/airsaqs. For more information about the Clean Air Status and Trends Network (CASTNET), visit http://www.epa.gov/castnet/.

Air Quality Where You Live

EPA has several Web sites to help answer frequently asked questions regarding local air quality. To see air quality trends for an individual area, visit the AirTrends Where You Live page at http://www.epa.gov/airtrends/where.html. Local trends are available at individual monitoring locations for pollutants monitored there.

To get air quality information to compare different areas of the country, visit AirCompare at http://www.epa.gov/aircompare. Select up to 10 counties across the country and find out how many days in each county the air was unhealthy last year for a specific health concern (e.g., asthma). Also find out which are the worst months. The example below shows a comparison of seven counties near Atlanta, Ga.

Air Compare – Compare Air Quality of U.S. Cities

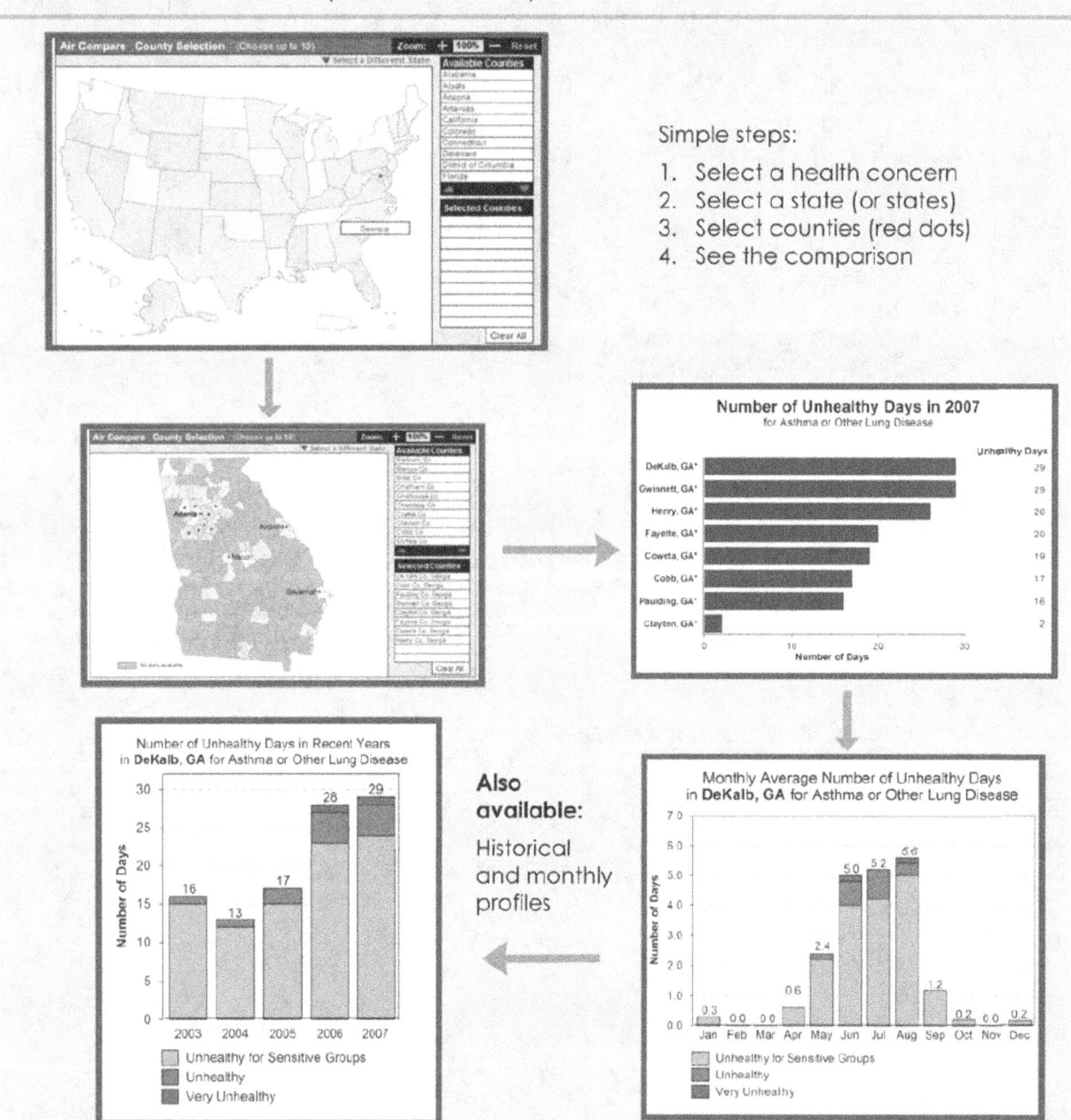

Simple steps:

1. Select a health concern
2. Select a state (or states)
3. Select counties (red dots)
4. See the comparison

Number of Unhealthy Days in 2007
for Asthma or Other Lung Disease

County	Unhealthy Days
DeKalb, GA*	29
Gwinnett, GA*	29
Henry, GA*	20
Fayette, GA*	20
Coweta, GA*	19
Cobb, GA*	17
Paulding, GA*	16
Clayton, GA*	2

Also available:

Historical and monthly profiles

Number of Unhealthy Days in Recent Years in **DeKalb, GA** for Asthma or Other Lung Disease

	2003	2004	2005	2006	2007
	16	13	17	28	29

- Unhealthy for Sensitive Groups
- Unhealthy
- Very Unhealthy

Monthly Average Number of Unhealthy Days in **DeKalb, GA** for Asthma or Other Lung Disease

Jan	Feb	Mar	Apr	May	Jun	Jul	Aug	Sep	Oct	Nov	Dec
0.3	0.0	0.0	0.6	2.4	5.0	5.2	5.6	1.2	0.2	0.0	0.2

- Unhealthy for Sensitive Groups
- Unhealthy
- Very Unhealthy

As of May 2008

PARTICLE POLLUTION

Particle pollution refers to two classes of particles based in part on long-established information on differences in sources, properties, and atmospheric behavior. EPA has set national standards to protect against the health and welfare effects associated with exposures to fine and coarse particles. Fine particles are generally referred to as those particles less than or equal to 2.5 micrometers (μm) in diameter, $PM_{2.5}$. PM_{10} (particles generally less than or equal to 10 μm in diameter) is the indicator used for the coarse particle standard.

TRENDS IN $PM_{2.5}$ CONCENTRATIONS

There are two national air quality standards for $PM_{2.5}$: an annual standard (15 μg/m^3) and a 24-hour standard (35 μg/m^3). Nationally, annual and 24-hour $PM_{2.5}$ concentrations declined by 9 and 10 percent, respectively, between 2001 and 2007, as shown in Figure 12.

Annual

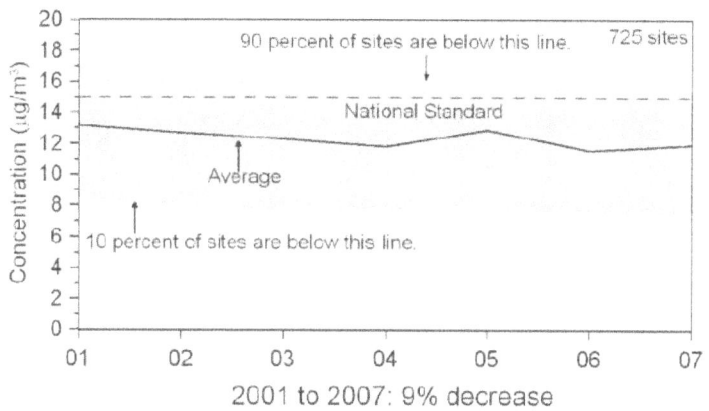

2001 to 2007: 9% decrease

24-hour

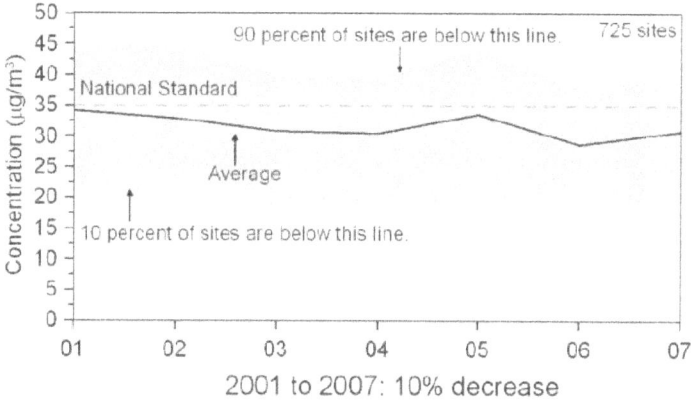

2001 to 2007: 10% decrease

Figure 12. National PM$_{2.5}$ air quality trends, 2001-2007 (annual and 24-hour average).

Note: In 2006, EPA revised the 24-hour standard from 65 to 35 μg/m^3.

The Great American Wood Stove Changeout

Residential wood burning in the U.S. emits 420,000 tons of particle pollution each year. EPA has partnered with the Hearth, Patio, and Barbecue Association, the American Lung Association and state, tribal, and local air quality agencies in the Great American Wood Stove Changeout. This partnership program provides homeowners with information and financial incentives to replace inefficient wood stoves with cleaner-burning gas, wood pellet, and EPA-certified wood stoves. This program can effectively reduce both particle pollution and toxic air pollutants, and help bring areas into attainment with the standards for $PM_{2.5}$.

As of October 2008, 7600 wood stoves and fireplaces have been replaced nationwide, eliminating close to 200 tons in annual particle pollution emissions, and achieving an estimated $100 million/year of health benefits.

For more information on wood stoves and the Great American Wood Stove Changeout, visit http://www.epa.gov/woodstoves/.

Participating Locations
- City/Urban Area
- Tribe
- County
- State

For each monitoring location, the maps in Figure 13 show whether annual and 24-hour $PM_{2.5}$ increased, decreased, or stayed about the same since the beginning of the decade. When comparing two 3-year periods, 2001-2003 and 2005-2007, almost all of the sites show a decline or little change in $PM_{2.5}$ concentrations. Several sites in California showed great improvement for both the 24-hour and annual $PM_{2.5}$ standards. One site in Pennsylvania also showed great improvement in the 24-hour $PM_{2.5}$ concentrations. Eighteen of the 618 sites showed an increase in annual $PM_{2.5}$ concentrations greater than 1 $\mu g/m^3$. These sites were located in Montana, Arizona, Texas, Arkansas, Louisiana, Alabama, South Carolina, Illinois, and Wisconsin. Of the 18 sites that showed an increase in annual $PM_{2.5}$ concentrations, only two (Birmingham and Houston) were above the

level of the annual $PM_{2.5}$ standard for the most recent year of data (2007). Fifty-eight sites showed an increase in 24-hour $PM_{2.5}$ concentrations greater than 3 $\mu g/m^3$. Of the 58 sites that showed an increase, 39 were below the level of the 24-hour $PM_{2.5}$ standard for the most recent year of data and 19 were above. The 19 sites above the standard were located in or near the following metropolitan areas: Birmingham, Ala.; Nogales, Ariz.; Chico, Calif.; Paducah, Ky.; Cincinnati, Ohio; Kalamath Falls, Ore.; Pittsburgh, Pa.; Clarksville, Tenn.; Provo, Utah; Green Bay, Wis.; Madison, Wis.; and Milwaukee, Wis. Due to the influence of local sources, it is possible for sites in the same general area to show opposite trends, as in the case of the Pittsburgh area for the 24-hour standard.

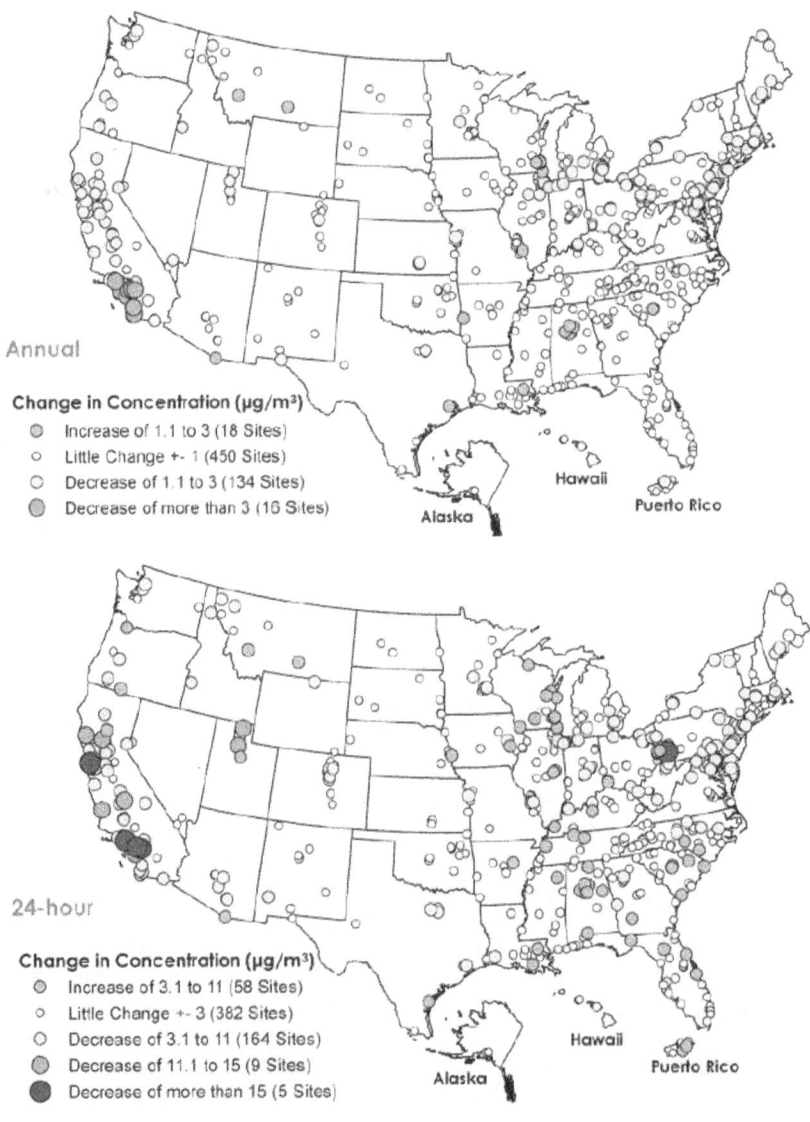

Figure 13. Change in $PM_{2.5}$ concentrations in $\mu g/m^3$, 2001-2003 vs. 2005-2007 (3-year average of annual and 24-hour average concentrations).

In 2007, the highest annual average PM$_{2.5}$ concentrations were in California, Arizona, Alabama, and Pennsylvania, as shown in Figure 14. The highest 24-hour PM$_{2.5}$ concentrations were in California, Idaho, and Utah. Even though California and Pennsylvania showed the greatest improvement since the start of the decade, they had some of the highest concentrations in 2007.

Some sites had high 24-hour PM$_{2.5}$ concentrations but low annual PM$_{2.5}$ concentrations, and vice versa. Sites that have high 24-hour concentrations but low or moderate annual concentrations exhibit substantial variability from season to season. For example, sites in the Northwest generally have low concentrations in warm months but are prone to much higher concentrations in the winter. Factors that contribute to the higher levels in the winter are extensive wood stove use coupled with prevalent cold temperature inversions that trap pollution near the ground. Nationally, more sites exceeded the level of the 24-hour PM$_{2.5}$ standard than exceeded the level of the annual PM$_{2.5}$ standard, as indicated by yellow and red dots on the maps below. About one-third of the sites that exceeded either standard exceeded both standards.

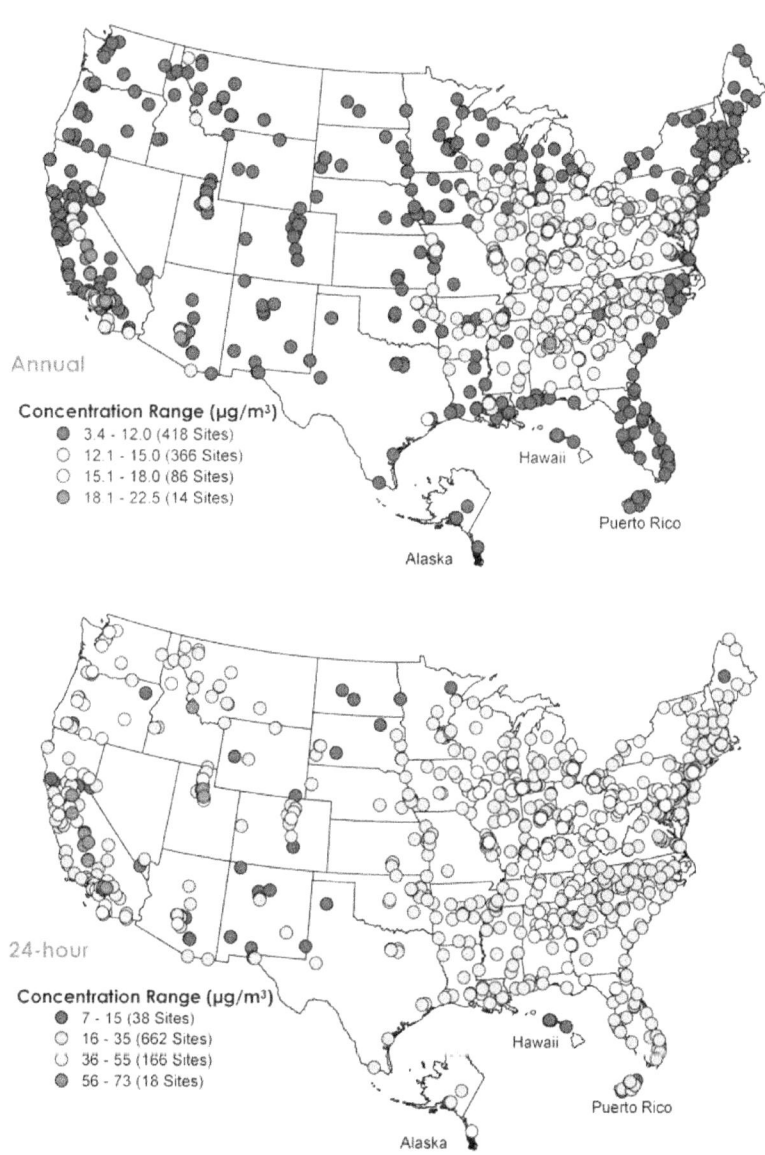

Figure 14. Annual average and 24-hour (98th percentile 24-hour concentrations) PM$_{2.5}$ concentrations in µg/m³, 2007.

WEATHER CONDITIONS INFLUENCE PM$_{2.5}$

As for ozone, in addition to emissions, weather plays an important role in the formation of PM$_{2.5}$. Figure 15 shows trends in PM$_{2.5}$ from 2001 through 2007, before and after adjusting for weather. PM$_{2.5}$ levels are monitored throughout the year, separate graphs are shown for the warm and cool months. After adjusting for weather, PM$_{2.5}$ concentrations have decreased by approximately 11 percent in both the warm and the cool season between 2001 and 2007. Weather influences during the warm season are generally larger than for the cool season, which is consistent with seasonal changes in emissions and temperature effects on the formation of secondary particle pollutants.

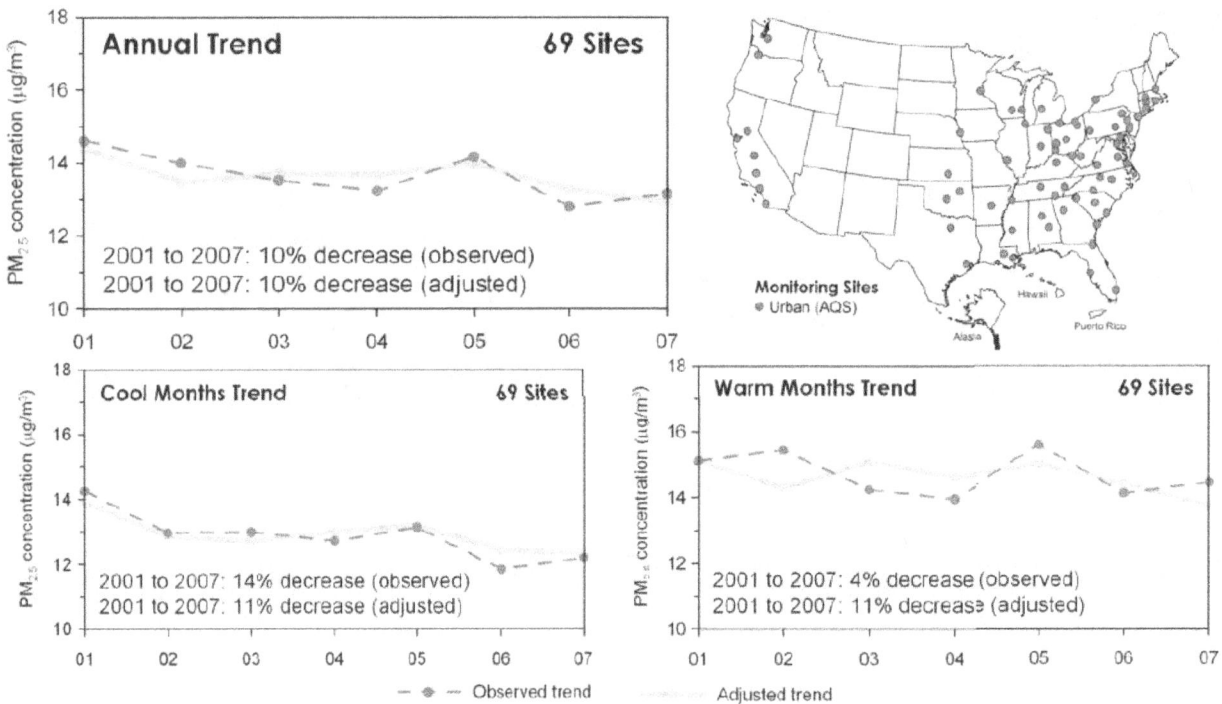

Figure 15. Trends in annual, cool months (October–April), and warm months (May–September) average PM$_{2.5}$ concentrations, before and after adjusting for weather, and the location of urban monitoring sites used in the average.

TRENDS IN PM$_{2.5}$ COMPOSITION 2002-2007

The mixture of different chemical components which make up PM$_{2.5}$ varies by season and location. This is true because of the differences in emissions and weather conditions that contribute to the formation and transport of PM$_{2.5}$. In general, PM$_{2.5}$ is primarily composed of sulfate, nitrate, organic carbon, and, to a lesser degree, elemental carbon and crustal material. Figure 16 shows regional trends in the composition of PM$_{2.5}$ from 2002 to 2007 for warm and cool months.

Sulfate levels are generally higher in the warm months and can account for the largest chemical component of PM$_{2.5}$ mass. Sulfate concentrations are their lowest in the Northwest. Also, the sulfate portion of PM$_{2.5}$ mass is lower in the Northwest than in any other region. Slight declines in sulfate levels are shown in the Northeast and Southeast during the cooler months. The highest sulfate concentrations appeared in the Southeast, Northeast, and Midwest during warm months of 2005, partly due to atypical weather conditions. The largest sources of sulfate in the eastern U.S. are SO$_2$ emissions from electric utilities and industrial boilers. In southern California and port cities in the Northwest, sulfates likely come from marine vessels.

Organic carbon is also a major component of PM$_{2.5}$ throughout the year in all regions. Organic carbon concentrations are highest in southern California and the Southeast. Organic carbon levels are the largest component of PM$_{2.5}$ in southern California and the Northwest during the cool months. Declines are shown year-round for southern California and during the warm months in the Northeast. The largest sources of organic carbon are VOCs and direct carbon emissions from highway vehicles, non-road mobile, waste burning, wildfires, and vegetation. In the western U.S., fireplaces and wood stoves are important contributors to organic carbon.

Nitrate concentrations are higher in the cool months than in the warm months. The lowest nitrate levels are in the Northeast and the Southeast. Nitrate levels have declined substantially in southern California and

slightly in all the other regions, except the Northwest, which shows no discernible trend. The largest sources of nitrates are NO_x emissions from highway vehicles, non-road mobile, electric utilities, and industrial boilers. Ammonia from sources such as fertilizer and animal feed operations contributes to the formation of sulfates and nitrates that exist in the air as ammonium sulfate and ammonium nitrate.

The remaining two components, elemental carbon and crustal material, are comparatively small but also exhibit some seasonal variability.

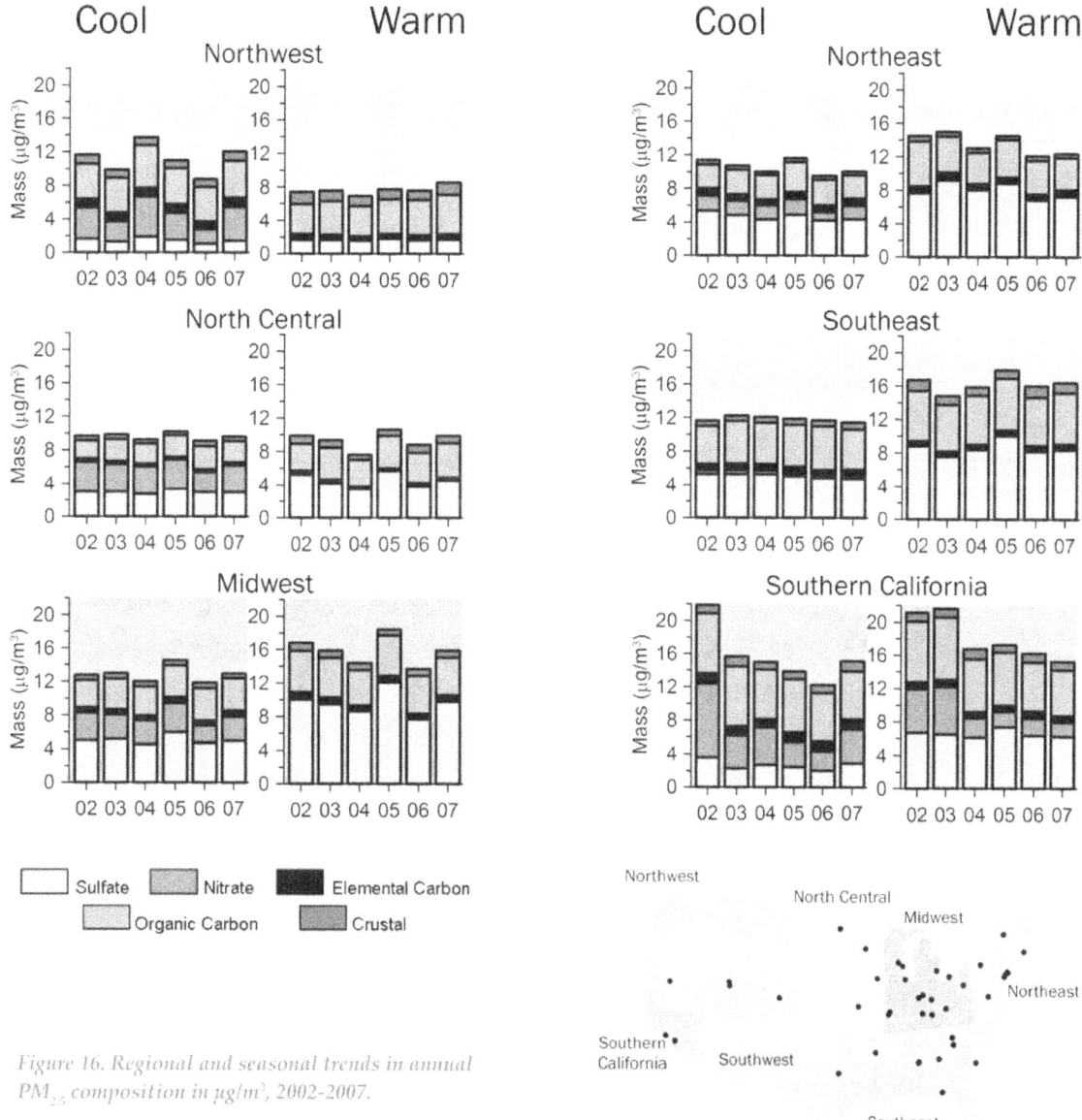

Figure 16. Regional and seasonal trends in annual PM$_{2.5}$ composition in µg/m³, 2002-2007.

Note: This figure is based on 42 monitoring locations with the most complete data from the national chemical speciation network for 2002-2007. There were no sites with complete data in the Southwest. For related information, read "Retained nitrate, hydrated sulfates, and carbonaceous mass in federal reference method fine particulate matter for six eastern U.S. cities," by N. H. Frank, *J. Air & Waste Manage. Assoc.* **56**, Pages 500-511, 2006.

TRENDS IN PM$_{10}$ CONCENTRATIONS

Nationally, 24-hour PM$_{10}$ concentrations declined by 21 percent between 2001 and 2007 as shown in Figure 17.

When comparing two 3-year periods, 2001-2003 and 2005-2007, most of the sites (nearly 90 percent) showed a decline or little change in PM$_{10}$ as shown in Figure 18. Twenty sites located in the Southwest, South Carolina, Missouri, and Wyoming showed a greater than 50 μg/m^3 decline. Seventy-four sites showed an increase of greater than 10 μg/m^3 over the trend period. Four of these sites (Houston, Texas; Rock Springs, Wyo.; Albany, Ga.; and Las Cruces, N.M.) showed large increases of 50 μg/m^3 or more.

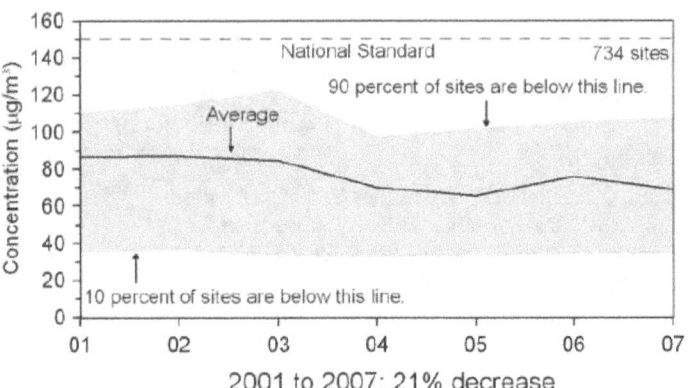

Figure 17. National PM$_{10}$ air quality trend, 2001-2007 (second maximum 24-hour concentration).

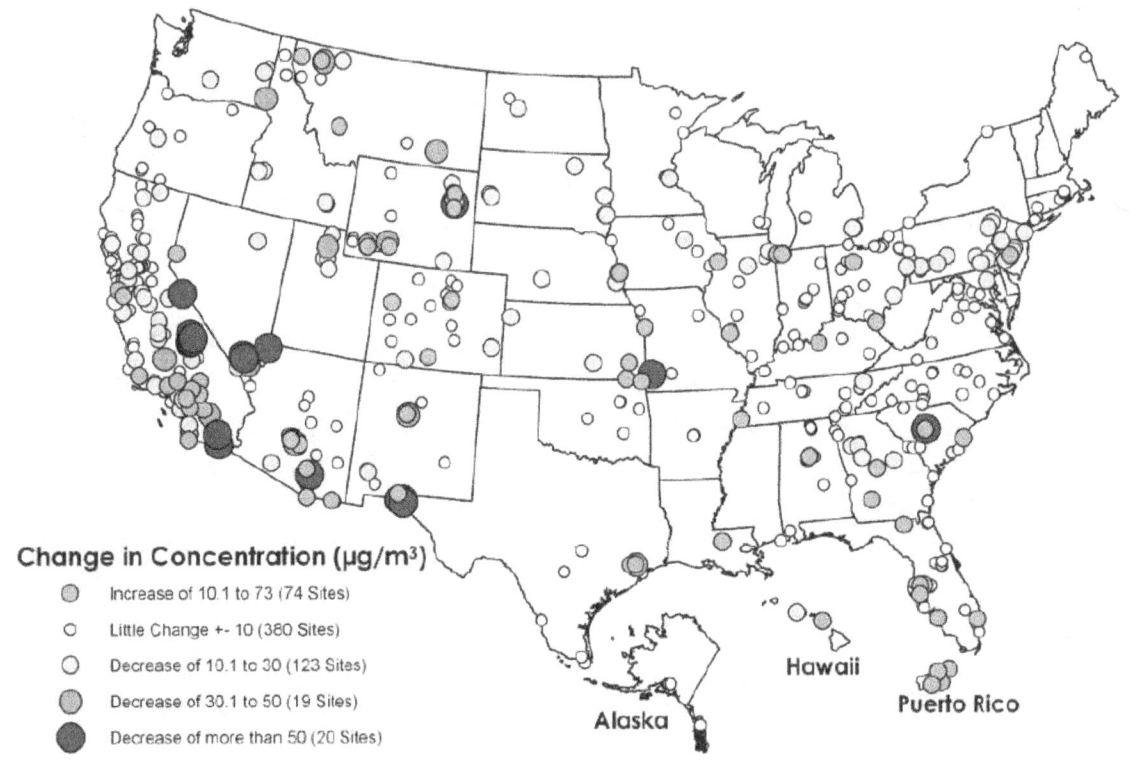

Figure 18. Change in PM$_{10}$ concentrations in μg/m^3, 2001-2003 vs. 2005-2007 (3-year average of annual average concentrations).

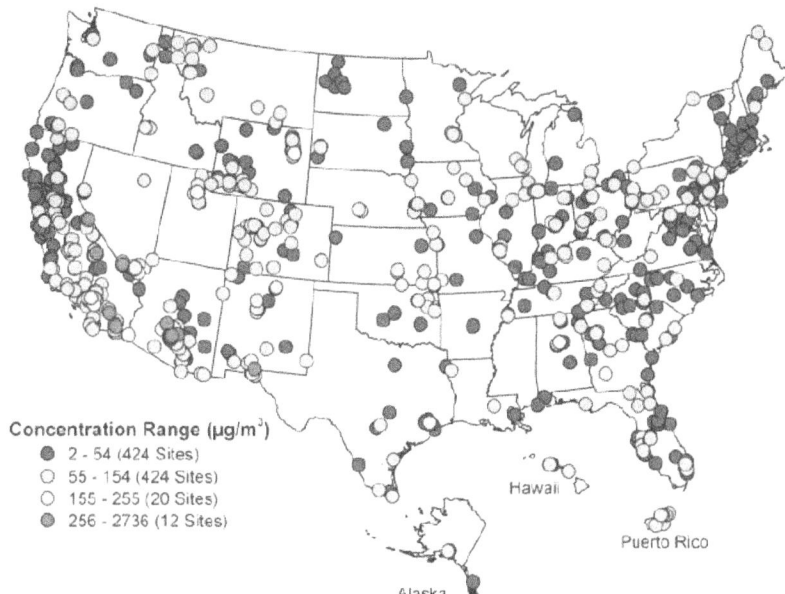

Figure 19 shows that in 2007, the highest PM_{10} concentrations were located in California, Nevada, Arizona, and New Mexico. This is also where some of the sites showed a greater than 50 µg/m³ decline. Highest concentrations are largely located in dry and/or industrial areas with high coarse particle sources.

Concentration Range (µg/m³)
- 2 - 54 (424 Sites)
- 55 - 154 (424 Sites)
- 155 - 255 (20 Sites)
- 256 - 2736 (12 Sites)

Hawaii

Puerto Rico

Alaska

Figure 19. PM_{10} concentrations in µg/m³, 2007 (second maximum 24-hour concentration).

Sustainable Skylines Initiative

EPA's Sustainable Skylines Initiative (SSI) is an innovative approach to achieve sustainable air quality and other environmental improvements including reducing the six common air pollutants, toxic air pollutants, and greenhouse gases. Participating cities may integrate transportation, energy, land use, and air quality planning efforts to achieve measurable emissions reductions within three years.

Sustainable Skylines

Each program is locally-driven, provides for collaboration among multiple stakeholders, identifies and leverages resources among public and private partners, and utilizes a consensus-based approach. Initiatives to encourage use of sustainable practices to help the air quality are already underway in Dallas, Texas; Kansas City, Kan.; and Missouri. EPA plans to have 10 cities in the program by the end of 2010.

Sustainable skyline projects include:

- Linking green building techniques with affordable housing initiatives.
- Decreasing the amount of heated surfaces within the central city.
- Increasing permeability of surfaces within the central city.
- Conducting pollution prevention audits for small businesses to reduce energy consumption and environmental impacts.
- Reducing landscape equipment emissions through sustainable lawn irrigation and turf management.
- Lowering vehicle emissions by increasing public transportation and reducing vehicle miles traveled
- Converting parking lots to parks.
- Reducing engine idling and applying retrofits to diesel engines.
- Retrofitting or replacing small off-road equipment to reduce emissions.

For more information about Dallas, visit http://www.sustainableskylines.org/Dallas/.

For more information about Kansas City, visit http://www.epa.gov/region7/citizens/ssi.htm.

LEAD

TRENDS IN LEAD CONCENTRATIONS

Nationally, concentrations of lead decreased 56 percent between 2001 and 2007, as shown in Figure 20. The national average concentrations shown are for 25 sites near large stationary sources and 78 sites that are not near stationary sources, 103 sites total. The typical average concentration near a stationary source (e.g., metals processors, battery manufacturers, and mining operations) is approximately 7 times the typical concentration at a site that is not near a stationary source. There are significant year-to-year changes in lead concentrations at sites near stationary sources; these reflect changes in emissions due to changes in operating schedules and plant closings. For example, lead concentrations declined between 2001 and 2002 mostly due to lower lead concentrations at sites in Herculaneum, Mo.

Figure 21 shows lead concentrations in 2007. Of the 109 sites shown, 25 exceeded the new lead standard (0.15 µg/m³). These sites are located in Alabama, Florida, Illinois, Indiana, Minnesota, Missouri, Ohio, Pennsylvania, Tennessee, and Texas. All of these sites are located near stationary lead sources. New requirements for monitoring near stationary lead sources will be implemented in 2010. Approximately 250 new locations will be monitoring lead concentrations.

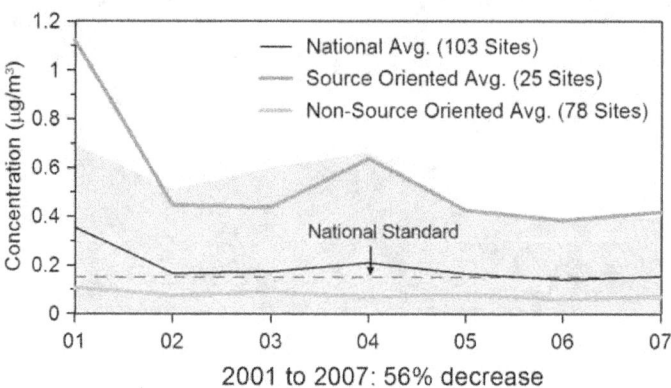

Figure 20. National lead air quality trend, 2001-2007 (maximum 3-month average).

Note: 90 percent of sites are shown in the yellow area.

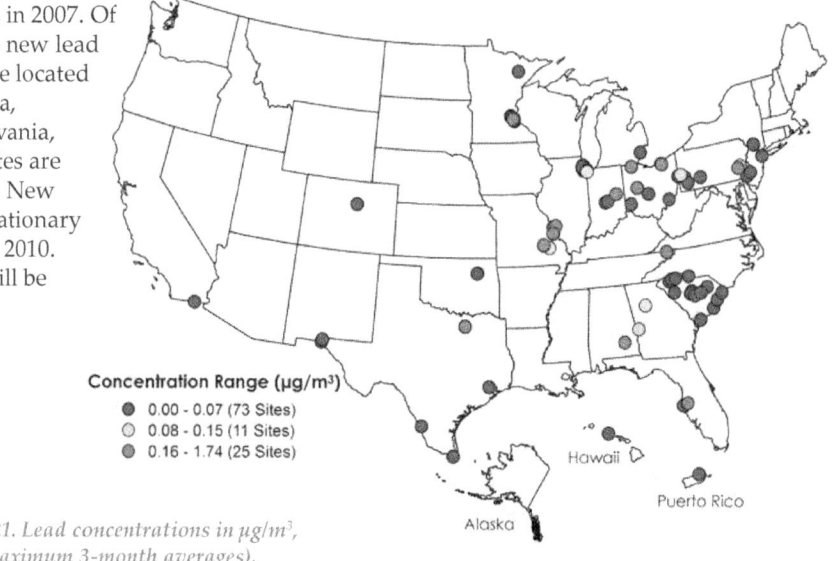

Figure 21. Lead concentrations in µg/m³, 2007 (maximum 3-month averages).

EPA Strengthens the National Ambient Air Quality Standards for Lead

On October 15, 2008, EPA strengthened the National Ambient Air Quality Standards for lead. The level for the previous lead standards was 1.5 µg/m³, not to be exceeded as an average for a calendar quarter, based on an indicator of lead in total suspended particles (TSP). The new standards, also in terms of lead in TSP, have a level of 0.15 µg/m³, not to be exceeded as an average for any three-month period within three years.

In conjunction with the revision of the lead standard, EPA also modified the lead air quality monitoring rules. Ambient lead monitoring is now required near lead emissions sources emitting 1 or more tons per year, and also in urban areas with a population equal to or greater than half a million people. Monitoring sites are required to sample every sixth day.

NO$_2$, CO, AND SO$_2$

TRENDS IN NO$_2$, CO, AND SO$_2$ CONCENTRATIONS

Nationally, concentrations of nitrogen dioxide (NO$_2$) decreased 20 percent between 2001 and 2007, as shown in Figure 22. In 2007, NO$_2$ concentrations were the lowest of the seven year period. All recorded concentrations were well below the level of the annual standard (0.053 ppm).

Figure 22. National NO$_2$ air quality trend, 2001-2007 (annual average).

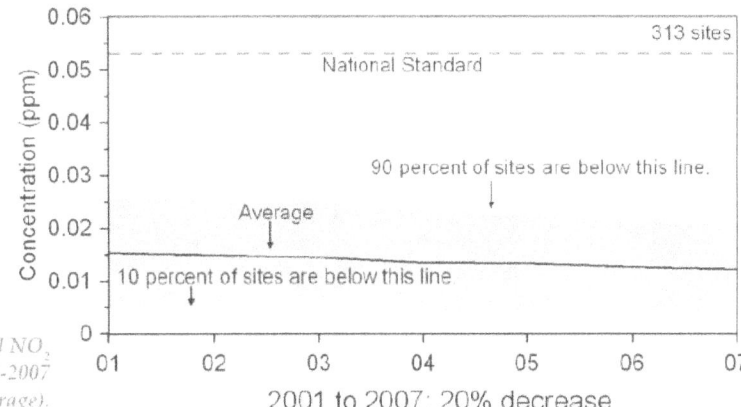

Nationally, concentrations of 8-hour carbon monoxide (CO) decreased 39 percent between 2001 and 2007, as shown in Figure 23. In 2007, CO concentrations were the lowest in the past seven years. All concentrations were below the 8-hour standard (9 ppm). One site near Salt Lake City, Utah, showed concentrations above the level of the 1-hour standard (35 ppm).

Figure 23. National CO air quality trend, 2001-2007 (second maximum 8-hour average).

Nationally, concentrations of sulfur dioxide (SO$_2$) decreased 24 percent between 2001 and 2007, as shown in Figure 24. In 2007, annual SO$_2$ concentrations were the lowest of the seven year period. All concentrations were below the level of the annual standard (0.03 ppm). One site in Hawaii showed concentrations above the level of the 24-hour standard (0.14 ppm), due to a nearby volcano.

Figure 24. National SO$_2$ air quality trend, 2001-2007 (annual average).

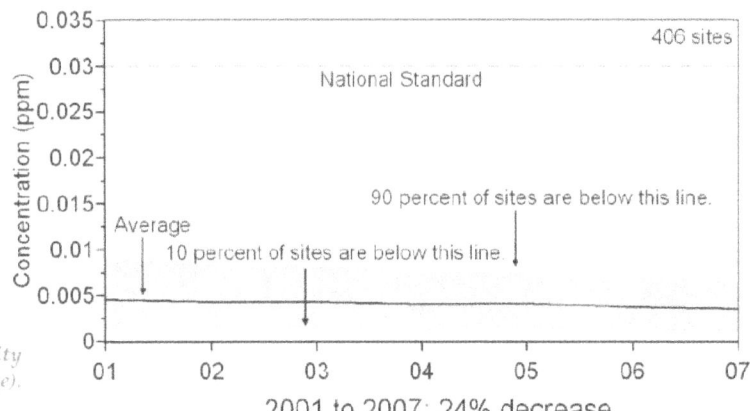

Downward trends in NO$_2$, CO, and SO$_2$ are the result of various national emissions control programs. Even though concentrations of these pollutants are low with respect to national standards, EPA continues to track these gaseous pollutants because of their contribution to other air pollutants (e.g., ozone and PM$_{2.5}$) and reduced visibility. National ambient air quality standards for these pollutants are under review.

TOXIC AIR POLLUTANTS

TRENDS IN TOXIC AIR POLLUTANT CONCENTRATIONS

Under the Clean Air Act, EPA regulates 187 toxic air pollutants. Toxicity levels, or the potential for adverse effects on human health, vary from pollutant to pollutant. For example, a few pounds of a relatively toxic pollutant may have a greater health effect than several tons of emissions of a less toxic pollutant. These toxicity levels can vary by orders of magnitude between pollutants. EPA has a recommended set of benchmark toxicity levels for estimating the effects of exposure to individual toxic air pollutants. For more information, visit http://www.epa.gov/ttn/atw/toxsource/table1.pdf.

Monitoring data are limited for most toxic air pollutants. Because ambient monitoring data is so limited for toxic air pollutants, EPA frequently relies on ambient modeling studies to better define trends in toxic air pollutants. One such modeling study, the National-Scale Air Toxic Assessment (NATA), is a nationwide study of ambient levels, inhalation exposures, and health risks associated with emissions of 177 toxic air pollutants (a subset of the Clean Air

Act's list of 187 toxic air pollutants). NATA examines individual pollutant effects as well as cumulative effects of many air pollutants on human health.

Figure 25 shows the estimated lifetime cancer risk across the continental U.S. by county based on 2002 NATA model estimates. The national average cancer risk level in 2002 is 36 in a million. Many urban areas as well as transportation corridors show a risk above the national average. From a national perspective, benzene is the most significant toxic air pollutant for which cancer risk could be estimated, contributing over 30 percent of the average individual cancer risk identified in the 2002 assessment. Though not included in the figure, exposure to diesel exhaust is also widespread. EPA has not adopted specific risk estimates for diesel exhaust but has concluded that diesel exhaust is a likely human carcinogen and ranks with the other substances that the national-scale assessment suggests pose the greatest relative risk to human health.

Figure 26 shows the trends in ambient monitoring levels for some of the important toxic air pollutants

Figure 25. Estimated county-level cancer risk from the 2002 National Air Toxics Assessment (NATA2002). Darker colors show greater cancer risk associated with toxic air pollutants.

identified by NATA. When the median percent change per year (marked by an x for each pollutant shown) is below zero, the majority of the sites in the U.S. are showing a decrease in concentrations. Ambient monitoring data show that for some of the toxic air pollutants of greatest widespread concern to public health (shown in yellow), 1,3-butadiene, benzene, tetrachloroethylene, and 1,4-dichlorobenzene concentration levels are declining at most sites. Concentrations of VOCs such as 1,3-butadiene, benzene, styrene, xylenes, and toluene decreased by approximately 5 percent or more per year at more than half of all monitoring sites. Concentrations of carbonyls such as formaldehyde, acetaldehyde, and propionaldehyde were equally likely to have increased or decreased. Chlorinated VOCs such as tetrachloroethylene, dichloromethane, and methyl chloroform decreased at more than half of all monitoring sites, but decreases among these species were much less consistent from site to site than among the other VOCs shown. Lead particles decreased in concentration at most monitoring sites; trends in other metals are less reliable due

to the small number of sampling sites available for analysis.

In 2003, in an effort to improve accuracy and geographic coverage of monitoring, EPA, working with its state and local partners, launched the National Air Toxics Trends Station (NATTS) program, a national monitoring network for toxic air pollutants. The principal objective of the NATTS network is to provide long-term monitoring data across representative areas of the country for NATA priority pollutants (e.g., benzene, formaldehyde, 1,3-butadiene, acrolein, and hexavalent chromium) in order to establish overall trends. The initial 23 stations were established between 2003 and 2005, two stations were added in 2007 and two more in 2008 for a total of 27 NATTS sites. In addition, the list of pollutants monitored was expanded to include polycyclic aromatic hydrocarbons (PAHs), of which naphthalene is the most prevalent.

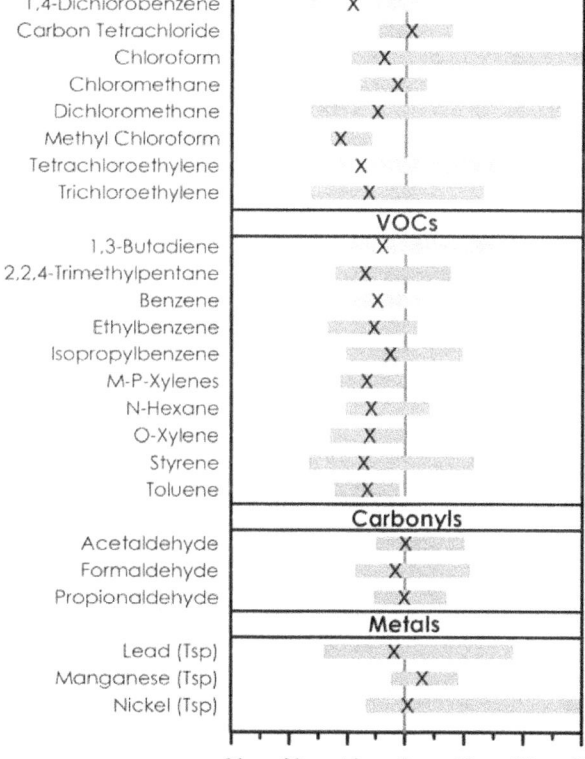

Figure 26. Distribution of changes in ambient concentrations at U.S. toxic air pollutant monitoring sites, 2000-2005 (percent change in annual average concentrations).
(Source: McCarthy M.C., Hafner H.R., Chinkin L.R., and Charrier J.G. [2007] Temporal variability of selected air toxics in the United States. Atmos. Environ. 41 [34], 7180-7194)

Notes: 10th and 90th percentiles are excluded if fewer than 10 monitoring sites were available for analyses. For chloroform and nickel, the 90th percentile percent changes per year are cut off at 30.

In addition to the NATTS program, about 300 monitoring sites are currently collecting data to help air pollution control agencies track toxic air pollutant levels in various locations around the country. State, local, and tribal air quality agencies operate these sites to address specific concerns such as areas of elevated concentrations or "hot spots," environmental justice concerns, and/or public complaints.

Figure 27 shows the locations of the toxic air pollutant monitoring sites. A majority of these sites are located in or near densely populated areas. Most sampling is conducted on a 1-in-6-day schedule for a 24-hour period. For more information about ambient air quality monitoring programs, visit http://www.epa.gov/ttn/amtic/.

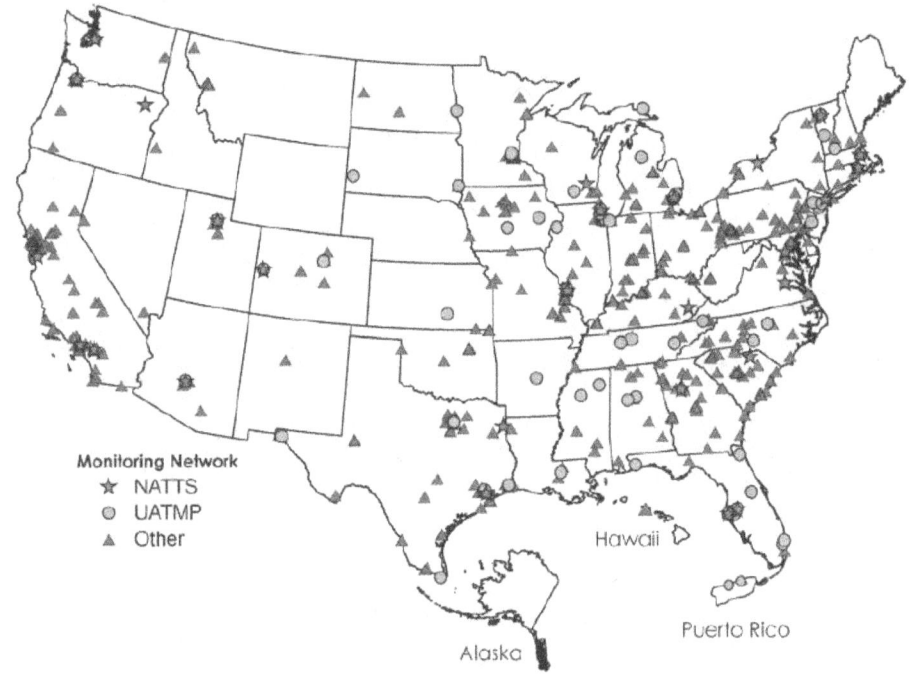

Figure 27. Toxic air pollutant monitoring sites operating in 2007 (by monitoring program).

Note: Some agencies use EPA-contracted sampling and laboratory analysis support services at the sites that are not NATTS program sites; these sites collectively are referred to as the Urban Air Toxics Monitoring Program (UATMP). At other monitoring sites, agencies perform their own laboratory analyses or use non-EPA contracted laboratories.

Local Short-term Toxic Air Pollutant Monitoring Projects

Due to the local nature of toxic air pollutant problems in 2004, EPA began funding local-scale monitoring projects. Typically these projects collect one to two years of monitoring data. To date, EPA has funded 51 projects and 25 have been completed.

The goal of local monitoring is to provide more flexibility to address middle- and neighborhood-scale (0.5 km to 4 km) issues that are not handled well by national networks. Objectives for these projects include:

- characterizing the degree and extent of local toxic air pollutant problems
- identifying and profiling local toxic air pollutant sources
- developing and assessing emerging measurement methods
- verifying the success of toxic air pollutant reduction activities

Results from these efforts are used to identify emission reduction options to be implemented at the local level.

Woodson site for the Hopewell Urban Air Toxics special study currently in progress located at Carter G. Woodson Middle School in Hopewell, Va. Apartment complexes can be seen in the background.

Detroit Exposure and Aerosol Research Study (DEARS)

A research study that the U.S. Environmental Protection Agency conducted in Detroit, Michigan, named the Detroit Exposure and Aerosol Research Study (DEARS), will help develop data that improves our understanding of human exposure to various air pollutants in our environment. The primary objective of DEARS was to compare air pollutant concentrations measured at central or community air monitoring stations with those measured in various neighborhoods in the Detroit, Michigan, area.

The study collected air quality samples over a three-year period (2004 through 2007) involving roughly 120 adults, randomly selected from among seven neighborhoods. These neighborhoods were selected because they represent a variation of potential industrial and regional source influences, housing type/age, and proximity to mobile emissions sources. Sampling included personal, indoor, backyard, and community monitors. Data were collected on particle pollution and toxic air pollutants.

These are the key questions to be addressed:

- How do air pollutant concentrations measured at community sites relate to those from residential indoor, outdoor, and personal monitoring?
- Can air pollutant concentrations monitored at community sites adequately represent estimates of what local residents are exposed to and the sources of these pollutants?

Participants engaged in five days of summertime monitoring and five days of wintertime monitoring per year. The summer and winter data collections provide important information on seasonal influences on pollutant concentrations and personal exposures to various sources.

Early findings indicate pollutant exposures may vary greatly among individuals living in the same area. The indoor air environment often highly influences individual exposures to some pollutant species, including those associated with volatile organic compounds and particle pollution. The movement of air into and out of the home was determined to be highly seasonal (nearly twice as high in the summer). This resulted in much higher exposures of individuals to particle pollution formed outside during the summer as compared to the winter. And, while the outdoor environment was a significant contributor of pollutants to local air quality outside homes close to major roadways, the impact of mobile-source related pollutants on air quality as a function of distance to the roadway was clearly evident. The impact of mobile-source related pollutants on air quality fell to near-background levels as distances from the roadway approached 300 meters.

(Source: http://www.epa.gov/dears/, photos courtesy of EPA)

Monitoring Methods

Personal Monitoring

Indoor Monitoring

Backyard Monitoring

Community Monitoring

TRENDS IN ATMOSPHERIC DEPOSITION

Pollution in the form of acids and acid-forming compounds (such as sulfur dioxide [SO_2] and oxides of nitrogen [NO_x]) can deposit from the atmosphere to the Earth's surface. Between the 1989-1991 and 2005-2007 time periods, sulfate deposition decreased over 30 percent in the Northeast and the Midwest, as shown in Figure 28. In addition, nitrate deposition decreased by about 30 percent in the Mid-Atlantic and Northeast, and 20 percent in the Midwest. These reductions have led to improving water quality in lakes and streams.

Most of these improvements are due to reductions in SO_2 and NO_x emissions from electric utilities and industrial boilers. The Acid Rain Program and the NO_x SIP Call in the East have led to significant reductions in SO_2 and NO_x emissions.

- SO_2 emissions have been reduced by more than 6.7 million tons from 1990 levels, or about 43 percent. Compared to 1980 levels, SO_2 emissions from power plants have dropped by more than 8 million tons, or about 48 percent. In 2007, annual SO_2 emissions fell by over 400,000 tons from 2006 levels.

- NO_x emissions have been reduced by about 3 million tons from 1990 levels, so that emissions in 2007 were less than half the level anticipated without the Acid Rain and NO_x SIP Call programs.

Ongoing review of the NO_2 and SO_2 secondary standards, which is scheduled to be completed in 2010, is addressing residual atmospheric deposition.

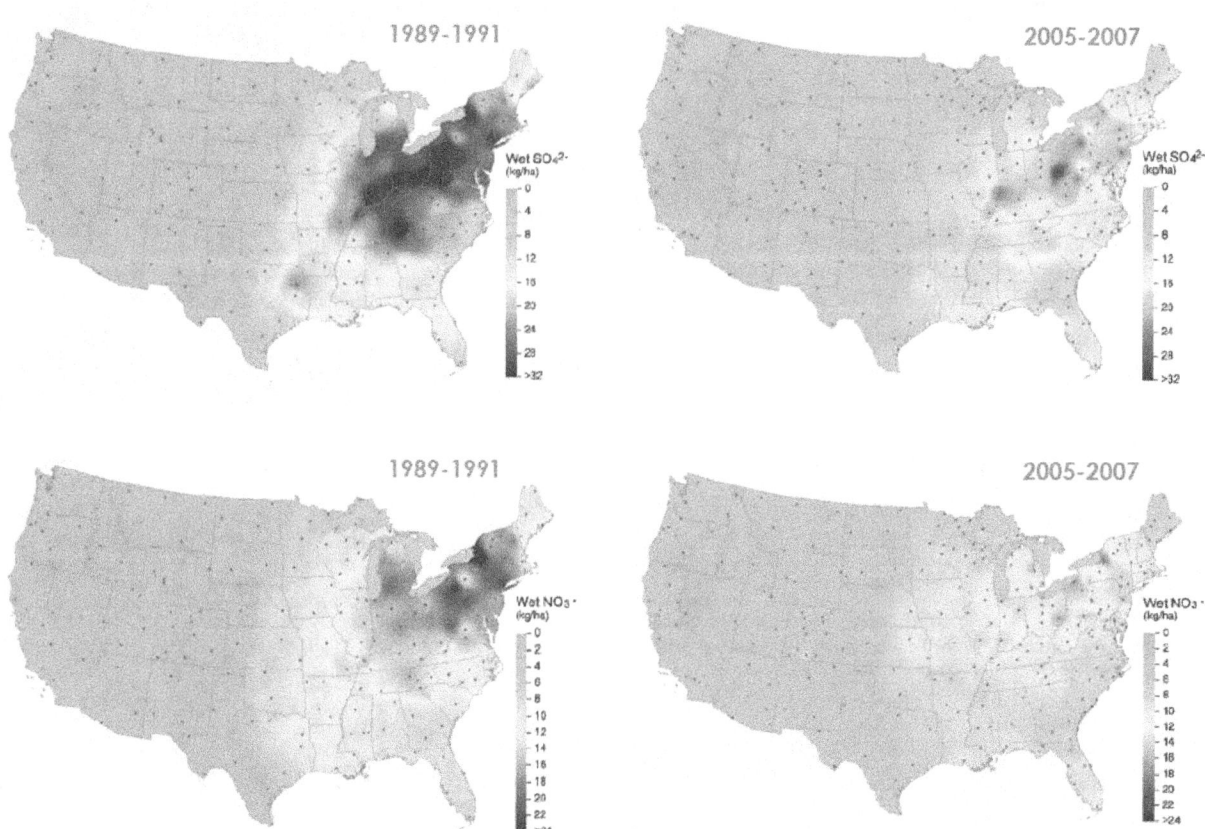

Figure 28. Three-year average deposition of sulfate (wet SO_4^{2-}) and nitrate (wet NO_3^-) in 1989-1991 and 2005-2007. Dots show monitoring locations. (Data source: National Atmospheric Deposition Program, http://nadp.sws.uiuc.edu/)

Mercury in the Environment

Mercury does not naturally occur as pure "quicksilver" but usually occurs as its principal ore cinnabar (HgS), one of 25 mercury-containing minerals that make up about 0.5 parts per million of the Earth's crust. Mercury is used in industry, commerce, mining, metallurgy, manufacturing, medicine, and dentistry. Human sources of atmospheric mercury include by-products of coal combustion, municipal and medical waste incineration, mining of metals for industry, and many others. Natural sources of atmospheric mercury include out-gassing from volcanoes and geothermal vents, and evaporation from naturally enriched soils, wetlands, and oceans. Atmospheric mercury concentrations can vary greatly depending on the location. Away from sources, elemental mercury concentrations are normally about 1.4 to 1.6 ng/m³ and reactive gaseous and particle-bound mercury concentrations are normally below 0.05 ng/m³. Close to sources, and in unique environments, concentrations can range widely, from 0.1 to over 100 ng/L in some outliers. Wet deposition could be responsible for 50-90 percent of mercury loading to many inland water bodies.

Mercury in the air is usually of little direct concern. But when mercury is washed from the air by precipitation into our streams and lakes, it is transformed into highly toxic methyl-mercury that can build up in fish. People are then exposed to mercury by eating fish.

Tracking progress and results is a critical step in understanding mercury in the environment. Since 1996, the Mercury Deposition Network (MDN) provides measurements of the amount of mercury in precipitation; the network now has more than 100 sites. In 2006 the highest levels of mercury wet deposition are shown in the eastern U.S. Between 1996 and 2005, significant decreases in mercury wet deposition were found at about half of 49 selected sites. Several sites in the mid-Atlantic and northeast show decreases greater than 1.5 percent.

Through the National Atmospheric Deposition Program efforts are underway to develop and implement additional mercury monitoring, specifically to characterize ambient mercury species and dry deposition (i.e., beyond MDN). For more information, visit http://nadp.sws.uiuc.edu/.

Technologies used to remove NO_x, SO_x, and particles also reduce mercury emissions ("Control of Mercury Emissions from Coal-fired Electric Utility Boilers: Interim Report", EPA-600/R-01-109, April 2002).

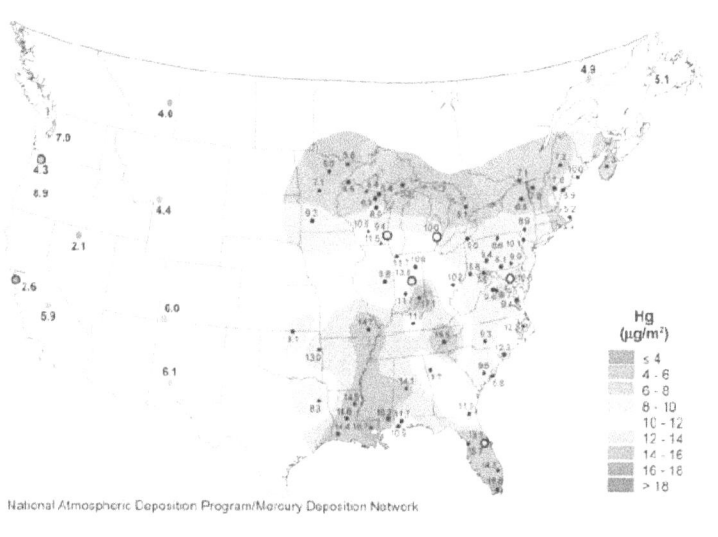

Hg (µg/m²)

≤ 4
4 - 6
6 - 8
8 - 10
10 - 12
12 - 14
14 - 16
16 - 18
> 18

National Atmospheric Deposition Program/Mercury Deposition Network

VISIBILITY IN SCENIC AREAS

TRENDS IN VISIBILITY

EPA monitors visibility trends in 155 of the 156 National parks and wilderness areas meeting the criteria established in the 1977 Clean Air Act amendments. Long-term trends in visibility on the annual 20 percent best and worst visibility days are shown in Figure 29. Most locations show improving visibility (decreasing haze) for the best visibility days, only Everglades National Park in Florida shows increasing haze. Five locations— Mt. Rainier National Park, Wash.; Great Smoky Mountains National Park, Tenn.; Great Gulf Wilderness, N.H.; Canyonlands National Park, Utah.; and Snoqualmie Pass, Wash.—show a notable decrease in haze for the worst days.

The Regional Haze Rule requires states to identify the most effective means of preserving conditions in these areas when visibility is at its best—based on the best 20 percent visibility days—and to gradually improve visibility when it is most impaired—based on the worst 20 percent visibility days. States are required to adopt progress goals for improving visibility, or visual range, from baseline conditions (represented by 2000 to 2004) to achieve natural background conditions within 60 years (represented by 2064). States determine whether they are meeting their goals by comparing visibility conditions from one five-year average to another (e.g., 2000-2004 to 2013-2017). The glide path to natural conditions in 2064 for the Shenandoah National Park is shown in Figure 30.

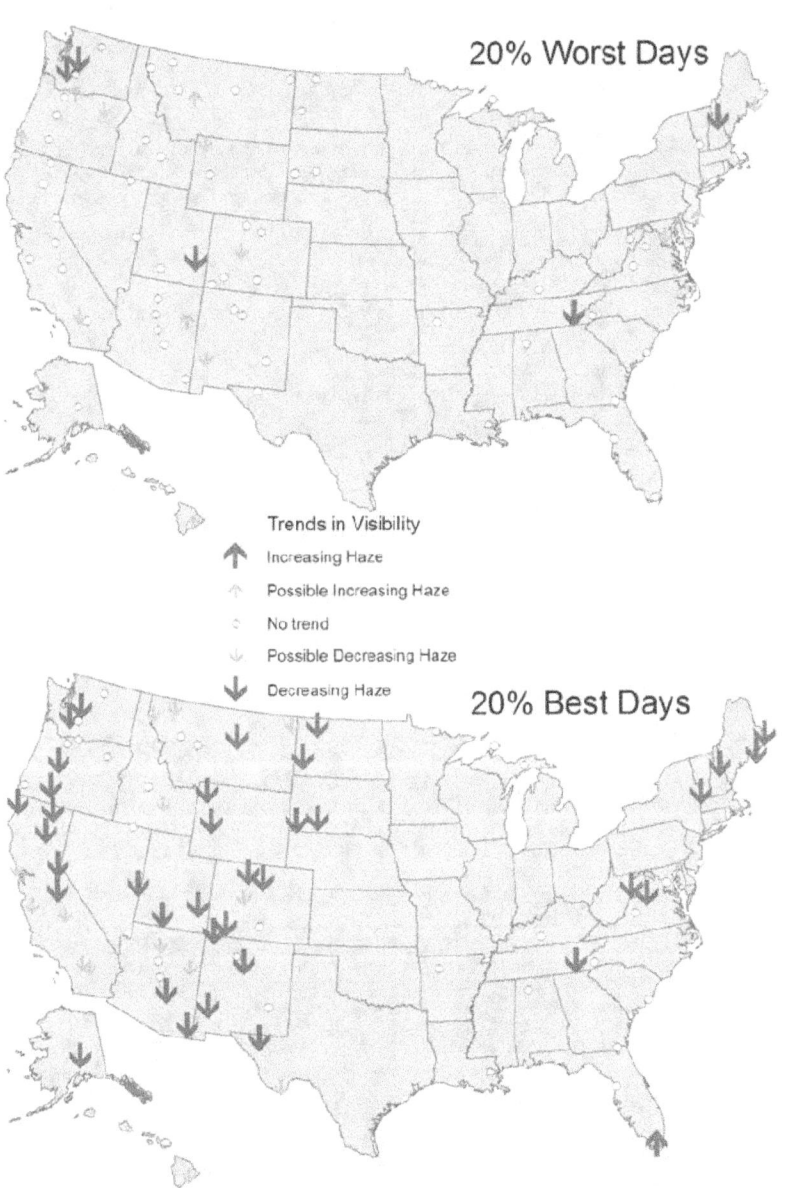

Figure 29. Trends in visibility on the 20 percent worst and best visibility days, 1996-2006.
(Source: http://www.nature.nps.gov/air/)

Note: Visibility trends using a haze index for the annual average for the 20 percent best and worst visibility days are based on aerosol measurements collected at Interagency Monitoring of Protected Visual Environments (IMPROVE) monitoring sites. The haze index is measured in deciviews (dv), a visibility metric based on the light extinction coefficient that expresses incremental changes in perceived visibility. Sites having at least six years of complete data were used to compute the change in dv per year over the trend period and its statistical significance.

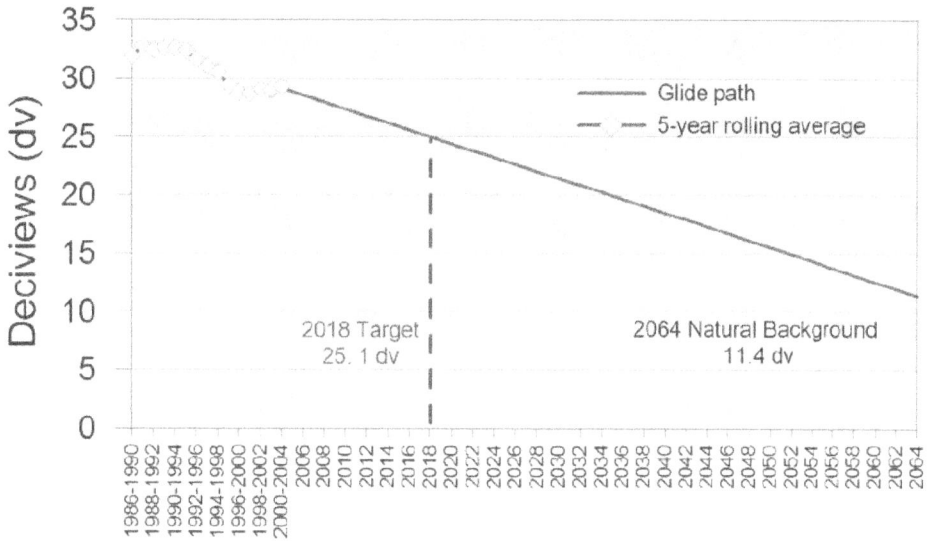

Figure 30. Glide path to natural conditions in 2064 for Shenandoah (deciviews).
(Source: Visibility Improvement State and Tribal Association of the Southeast — VISTAS)

Notes: A change of one deciview is a change in visibility that is descernable. The figure shows a 5-year rolling average for the 20 percent worst visibility days.

Visibility at Great Smoky Mountains National Park

Visibility at Great Smoky Mountains National Park for the 20 percent haziest days in the baseline period 2000-2004 (30.3 deciviews) was among the poorest in the country. However, projected improvements in visibility in the Southern Appalachian Mountains, such as the Great Smoky Mountains, are among the largest in the country. Ammonium sulfate is the major contributor to haze in the southeastern U.S. There has been a small but significant reduction in sulfate and corresponding improvement in visibility at Great Smoky Mountains National Park between 1990 and 2004. These improvements are due primarily to SO_2 emissions reductions under the Acid Rain Title IV provisions of the 1990 Clean Air Act Amendments.

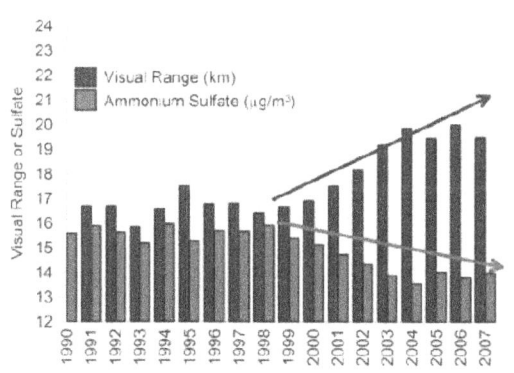

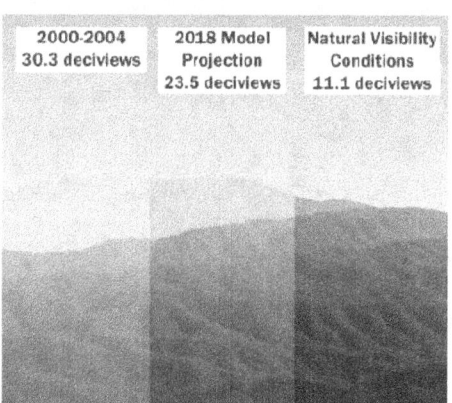

| 2000-2004 30.3 deciviews | 2018 Model Projection 23.5 deciviews | Natural Visibility Conditions 11.1 deciviews |

Visibility Improvement State and Tribal Association of the Southeast (VISTAS) modeling projects that emissions reductions under existing state and federal regulations will significantly improve visibility by 2018. The uniform rate of progress for improving visibility between baseline conditions and natural background would mean visibility of 25.8 deciviews in 2018; modeling indicates that visibility in 2018 will be 23.5 deciviews, better than the uniform rate of progress, and is a 6.8 deciview improvement compared to baseline conditions (2000-2004). Natural visibility conditions on the 20 percent haziest days at Great Smoky Mountains National Park are projected to be 11.1 deciviews. Considerable additional progress is needed to achieve natural visibility.

(Source: Images from WinHaze Visual Air Quality Model, Air Resource Specialists, Inc. and Jim Renfro, Great Smoky Mountains National Park)

CLIMATE CHANGE AND AIR QUALITY

CLIMATE AND AIR QUALITY

Climate and air pollution are closely coupled. Ground-level ozone absorbs solar radiation, and thus contributes to increases in global temperature. Particle pollution scatters or absorbs solar radiation and changes cloud formation processes and the amount of cloud cover. The net effect of particle pollution is cooling as scattering generally dominates.

Changes in climate affect air quality. Warming of the atmosphere increases the formation of ground-level ozone, while the overall directional impact of climate change on particle pollution in the U.S. remains uncertain.

Because of these links between climate and air quality, the National Academy of Sciences recommends that air pollution and climate change policies be developed through an integrated approach. A number of strategies being discussed for climate—energy efficiency, renewable energy, and reducing the number of vehicles on the highway will provide reductions in emissions that contribute to multiple air quality concerns such as ozone and particle pollution, toxic air pollutants, atmospheric deposition, and visibility.

TRENDS IN GREENHOUSE GAS EMISSIONS AND CLIMATE

EPA, in collaboration with other government agencies, tracks both changes in climate and changes in greenhouse gas emissions. Figure 31 shows the trends in domestic greenhouse gas emissions over time in the U.S. The dominant gas emitted is carbon dioxide (mostly from fossil fuel combustion). Total U.S. greenhouse gas emissions increased 15 percent between 1990 and 2006.

A number of EPA scientists participate on the Intergovernmental Panel on Climate Change (IPCC), an international scientific body that provides information about the causes of climate change and its potential effects on the environment. In a series of comprehensive reports completed in 2007, the IPCC concludes that "warming of the climate system is unequivocal, as is now evident from observations of increases in global average air and ocean temperatures, widespread melting of snow and ice, and rising global average sea level." Average global temperatures have been rising and the IPCC reports an increasing rate of warming over the last 25 years.

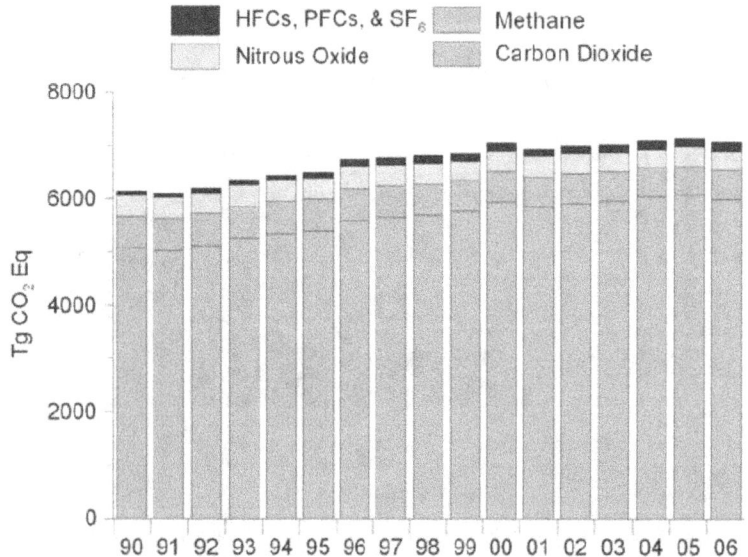

Figure 31. Domestic greenhouse gas emissions in teragrams of carbon dioxide equivalents (Tg CO_2 eq), 1990-2006. (Source: http://epa.gov/climatechange/emissions/usinventoryreport.html)

Notes: A teragram is equal to 1 million metric tons. Emissions in the figure include fluorocarbons (HFCs, PFCs) and sulfur hexafluoride (SF_6).

CHANGES IN CLIMATE AFFECT AIR QUALITY

Due to the warming, the IPCC projects with virtual certainty "declining air quality in cities." In summarizing the impact of climate change on ozone and particle pollution, the IPCC concludes that "future climate change may cause significant air quality degradation by changing the dispersion rate of pollutants, the chemical environment for ozone and particle pollution generation, and the strength of emissions from the biosphere, fires, and dust." Large uncertainties remain, limiting our ability to provide a quantitative description of the interactions between air quality and climate change. However, as noted in the following two examples, research is under way that will provide an improved understanding of these connections.

Using estimates from a computer model that assumes continued growth in global GHG emissions, a study cited in the 2007 IPCC report shows how ground-level ozone in the New York metropolitan area may increase from current levels given future climate change. Figure 32 shows this study projects daily 1-hour ozone increases of 0.0003 to 0.0043 ppm across the region due to climate change alone in the 2050s compared to the 1990s.

Pollutants from forest fires can affect air quality for thousands of miles. The IPCC reported that in North America wildfires are increasing and in a warmer future are likely to intensify with drier soils and longer growing seasons. Figure 33 shows increases in the annual frequency of large (>100,000 hectares) western U.S. forest wildfires (bars) associated with the mean March through August temperature. In the last three decades, the wildfire season in the western U.S. has increased by 78 days in response to a spring-summer warming of 0.87°C.

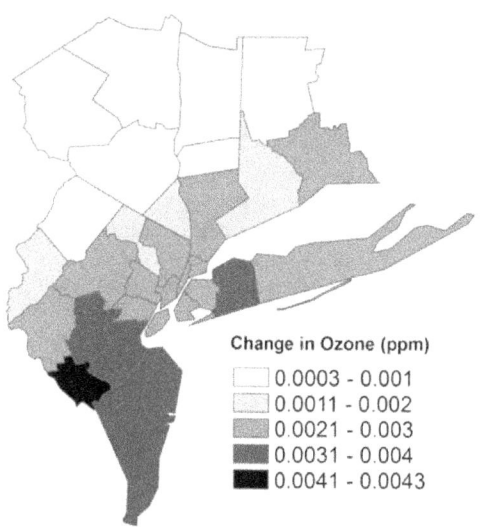

Change in Ozone (ppm)
- 0.0003 - 0.001
- 0.0011 - 0.002
- 0.0021 - 0.003
- 0.0031 - 0.004
- 0.0041 - 0.0043

Figure 32. Estimated changes in 1-hour daily maximum ozone concentrations (ppm) in the 2050s compared with those in the 1990s for the New York metropolitan area, under scenario M1 in which climate change alone drives changes in air quality.

(Source: Knowlton K., et al. [2004] Assessing ozone-related health impacts under a changing climate. Environ. Health. Perspect., 112: 1557-1563)

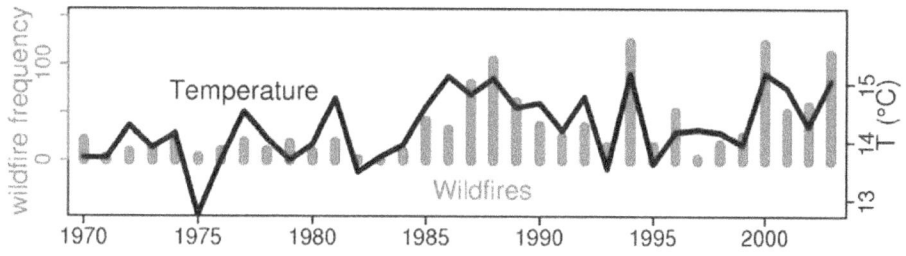

Figure 33. Frequency of Western U.S. forest wildfires compared to spring-summer temperature.
(Source: Westerling A.L., et al. [2006] Warming and earlier spring increase western U.S. forest wildfire activity. Science, 313: 940-943)

INTERNATIONAL TRANSPORT OF AIR POLLUTION

INTERNATIONAL TRANSPORT OF AIR POLLUTION

While domestic sources of emissions are the primary cause of most air pollution in our country, the U.S. is both a source of pollution and a receiver of pollution from other countries. Air pollution flows across boundaries—not only between the U.S. and our closest neighbors, Canada and Mexico, but also between North America, Europe, and Asia, and to some extent, between North America, Africa, and Central and South America. International flow of air pollutants into the U.S. contributes to observed concentrations of ozone and particle pollution and deposition of mercury, persistent organic pollutants (POPs), and acid deposition.

TRANSPORT OF AIR POLLUTION AFFECTS THE U.S.

The impact that international transport of air pollution has on our ability to attain air quality standards or other environmental objectives in the U.S. has yet to be characterized (except in areas that are downwind

of cities or sources in Mexico or Canada). Figure 34 illustrates major intercontinental transport pathways. Estimates based on the available evidence are highly uncertain, but suggest that the current contributions of international transport to observed concentrations, acid deposition and deposition of mercury are small. Increased emissions of particle pollution, mercury, and ozone precursors in developing countries associated with economic growth may increase background levels of these pollutants in the U.S.

For ozone and particle pollution, increased background levels of these pollutants could potentially make it more difficult for local and regional areas to achieve the National Ambient Air Quality Standards and long-term visibility improvement goals. Transported ozone and particle pollution also contribute to radiative forcing and global and regional climate change. For mercury and POPs, international flows contribute to deposition, and eventual human and ecosystem chemical exposures. In some locations, especially in Alaska, international sources are the dominant source of contamination for these toxic air pollutants.

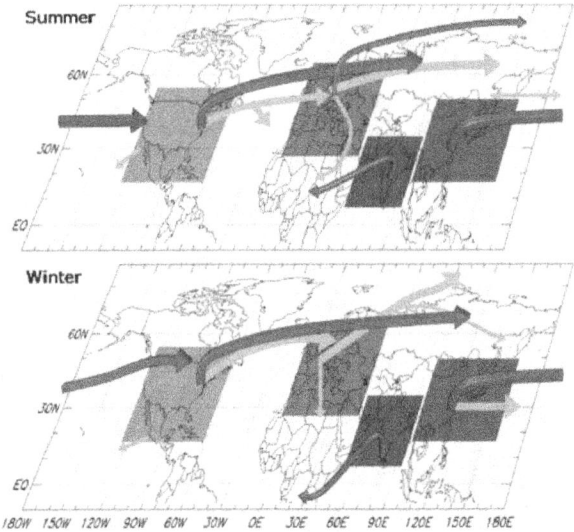

Figure 34. Major intercontinental transport pathways of CO emissions in the Northern Hemisphere. The colored boxes indicate the four source and receptor regions used in the Task Force on Hemispheric Transport of Air Pollution's (HTAP) on-going model intercomparison study. The arrows approximate the magnitude of main transport pathways in summer (June, July, August) and winter (December, January, February), based on modelled average CO transport over 8–10 day periods. Light arrows indicate transport generally near ground level (less than 3 km above the surface) and dark arrows indicate transport higher in the atmosphere (more than 3 km above the surface).
(Source: Figure E-1, HTAP 2007. Adapted from Figure 2 of Stohl and Eckhardt [2004], with kind permission of Springer Science and Business Media)

International Efforts to Address Air Pollution Transport

EPA is involved in a number of international efforts to address air pollution transport, including:

- Reducing transborder air pollution transport, visit http://www.epa.gov/airmarkets/progsregs/usca/index.htm

- Understanding intercontinental transport in the northern hemisphere, visit http://www.htap.org

- Addressing global scale transport, visit http://chm.pops.int and http://www.chem.unep.ch/mercury/new_partnership.htm

- Building cooperative relationships to improve air quality and reduce long-range transport of air pollution in key countries, visit http://www.epa.gov/oia/regions/

Shipping and Aviation Emissions

Shipping and aviation are two of the fastest growing sources of emissions globally, with important consequences for air quality. Emissions from both sectors have received increased attention and the International Maritime Organization recently acted to strengthen emissions controls on ocean-going ships.

EFFORTS TO BETTER UNDERSTAND TRANSPORT OF AIR POLLUTION

EPA and other agencies are working via treaties and international cooperative efforts to address the international transport of air pollution. Since 2001, EPA has led collaborative efforts among many of the leading U.S. researchers in the global atmospheric chemistry community to improve our understanding of trans-Pacific and trans-Atlantic transport. EPA and the European Commission co-chair the Task Force on Hemispheric Transport of Air Pollution, a multinational effort to better understand the soures, transport, and impacts of air pollution in the northern hemisphere. In 2008, EPA, with contributions from NOAA, NASA, and the National Science Foundation (NSF), has sponsored a National Academy of Sciences study to examine the significance of the international transport of air pollutants for air quality, atmospheric deposition, and climate change.

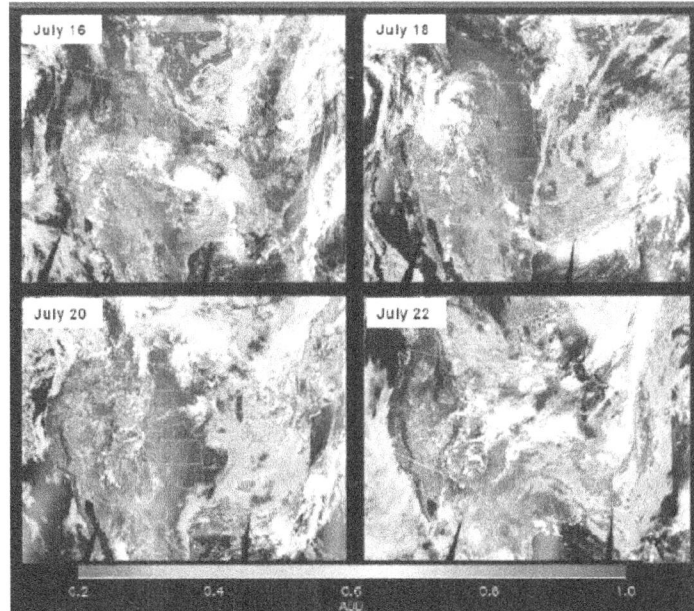

Tracking Air Pollutant Transport with Satellites

During the 2004 summer, the largest Alaskan wild fire event on record occurred in late June-July and consumed 2.72 million hectares of boreal forest. The figure shows aerosol optical depth (AOD) data from the Moderate Resolution Imaging Spectroradiometer (MODIS) instrument aboard the Terra satellite for a series of days in July 2004. The MODIS AOD is plotted over the MODIS Terra true color image for each day. This series of days shows high aerosol concentrations (in red) associated with long-range transport of the Alaskan wild fire plume as it crosses over the northern border of the U.S. on July 16. This aerosol plume travelled south-eastward behind the cold front (evident in the clouds captured in the MODIS true color image) over the following days, eventually affecting surface $PM_{2.5}$ levels along the Eastern U.S.

Aerosol optical depth (AOD) measurements for a series of days in July 2004. (Image provided by J. Szykman, EPA, and C. Kittaka, SSAI-NASA/LaRC)

TERMINOLOGY

AQI	Air Quality Index
AQS	Air Quality System
AOD	aerosol optical depth
CAA	Clean Air Act
CASTNET	Clean Air Status and Trends Network
CCSP	U.S. Climate Change Science Program
CO	carbon monoxide
dv	deciviews
EC	elemental carbon
EPA	U.S. Environmental Protection Agency
FRM	Federal Reference Method
GHG	greenhouse gas
HFCs	hydrofluorocarbons
HTAP	Hemispheric Transport of Air Pollution
IMPROVE	Interagency Monitoring of Protected Visual Environments
MODIS	Moderate Resolution Imaging Spectroradiometer
NAAQS	National Ambient Air Quality Standards
NASA	National Aeronautics and Space Administration
NATTS	National Air Toxics Trends Stations
NEI	National Emissions Inventory
NH_3	ammonia
NO	nitric oxide
NO_x	oxides of nitrogen
NO_2	nitrogen dioxide
NSF	National Science Foundation
O_3	ground-level ozone
Pb	lead
PFCs	perfluorinated compounds
PM	particulate matter
$PM_{2.5}$	particulate matter (fine) 2.5 μm or less in size
PM_{10}	particulate matter 10 μm or less in size
POP	persistent organic pollutants
ppm	parts per million
SF_6	sulfur hexafluoride
SIP	state implementation plan
SO_x	sulfur oxides
SO_2	sulfur dioxide
UATMP	Urban Air Toxics Monitoring Program
μm	micrometers
μg/m^3	micrograms per cubic meter
VOC	volatile organic compound

Atmospheric Deposition

Acid Rain Program: http://www.epa.gov/airmarkets/progsregs/arp/index.html

Acid Rain Program 2006 Progress Report: http://www.epa.gov/airmarket/progress/arp06.html

National Atmospheric Deposition Program: http://nadp.sws.uiuc.edu/

Background/General Information

Air Quality Index: http://www.airnow.gov

Air Quality System: http://www.epa.gov/ttn/airs/airsaqs/

EPA's Clean Air Research Program: http://www.epa.gov/ord/npd/cleanair-research-intro.htm

EPA-Funded Particulate Matter Research Centers:

http://cfpub.epa.gov/ncer_abstracts/index.cfm/fuseaction/outlinks.centers#19

Framework for Assessing the Public Health Impacts of Risk Management Decisions:

http://www.epa.gov/ORD/npd/hhrp/files/hhrp-framework.pdf

Health and Ecological Effects: http://www.epa.gov/air/urbanair/

Multi-Ethnic Study of Atherosclerosis and Air Pollution (MESA Air): http://depts.washington.edu/mesaair/

National Ambient Air Quality Standards: http://www.epa.gov/air/criteria.html

National Center for Environmental Assessment: http://cfpub.epa.gov/ncea/

National Particle Components Toxicity (NPACT) Initiative: http://www.healtheffects.org/Pubs/NPACT.pdf

Office of Air and Radiation: http://www.epa.gov/air/

Office of Air Quality Planning and Standards: http://www.epa.gov/air/oaqps/

Office of Atmospheric Programs: http://www.epa.gov/air/oap.html

Office of Transportation and Air Quality: http://www.epa.gov/otaq/

Climate Change

Climate change: http://www.epa.gov/climatechange/

U.S. Climate Change Science Program: http://www.climatescience.gov

Emissions and trends in greenhouse gases:

http://www.epa.gov/climatechange/emissions/usinventoryreport.html

Green Car Congress: http://www.greencarcongress.com/2008/06/us-vehicle-mile.html

Intergovernmental Panel on Climate Change: http://www.ipcc.ch

Traffic Volume Trends: http://www.fhwa.dot.gov/ohim/tvtw/tvtpage.cfm

Emissions and Control Programs

Emissions: http://www.epa.gov/air/emissions/

NO_x Budget Trading Program/NO_x SIP Call: http://www.epa.gov/airmarkets/progsregs/nox/sip.html

Toxic Air Pollutants

1999 National-Scale Air Toxics Assessment: http://www.epa.gov/ttn/atw/nata1999/

Measurements and Trends

Air Quality Trends: http://www.epa.gov/airtrends/

Air Trends Design Values: http://www.epa.gov/air/airtrends/values.html

Clean Air Status and Trends Network (CASTNET): http://www.epa.gov/castnet/

EPA Monitoring Network: http://www.epa.gov/ttn/amtic/

Local air quality trends: http://www.epa.gov/airtrends/where.html

National Air Monitoring Strategy Information: http://www.epa.gov/ttn/amtic/monstratdoc.html

National Core Monitoring Network: http://www.epa.gov/ttn/amtic/ncore/index.html

Trends in ozone adjusted for weather conditions: http://www.epa.gov/airtrends/weather.html

Visibility

National Park Service: http://www.nature.nps.gov/air/

Regional Haze Program: http://www.epa.gov/visibility

Visibility Information Exchange Web System (VIEWS): http://vista.cira.colostate.edu/views/

International Transport

International Maritime Organization: http://www.imo.org

FAA's Aviation Climate Change Research Initiative (ACCRI):

http://www.faa.gov/about/office_org/headquarters_offices/aep/aviation_climate/

Task Force on Hemispheric Transport of Air Pollution: http://www.htap.org